RETIRE RIGHT

RETIRE RIGHT

■ ■ ■

The Retirement Docs' Proven Prescription for

Living a Happy, Fulfilling Rest of Your Life

FREDERICK T. FRAUNFELDER, M.D.

JAMES H. GILBAUGH JR., M.D.

Previously published as *Retirement RX*

AVERY ■ A MEMBER OF PENGUIN GROUP (USA) INC. ■ NEW YORK

AVERY

Published by the Penguin Group
Penguin Group (USA) Inc., 375 Hudson Street, New York, New York 10014, USA * Penguin Group
(Canada), 90 Eglinton Avenue East, Suite 700, Toronto, Ontario M4P 2Y3, Canada (a division of Pearson
Canada Inc.) * Penguin Books Ltd, 80 Strand, London WC2R 0RL, England * Penguin Ireland,
25 St Stephen's Green, Dublin 2, Ireland (a division of Penguin Books Ltd) * Penguin Group (Australia),
250 Camberwell Road, Camberwell, Victoria 3124, Australia (a division of Pearson Australia Group
Pty Ltd) * Penguin Books India Pvt Ltd, 11 Community Centre, Panchsheel Park, New Delhi–110 017, India *
Penguin Group (NZ), 67 Apollo Drive, Rosedale, North Shore 0632, New Zealand (a division
of Pearson New Zealand Ltd) * Penguin Books (South Africa) (Pty) Ltd,
24 Sturdee Avenue, Rosebank, Johannesburg 2196, South Africa

Penguin Books Ltd, Registered Offices: 80 Strand, London WC2R 0RL, England

First trade paperback edition 2009
Previously published in hardcover as *Retirement RX*

Most Avery books are available at special quantity discounts for bulk purchase for sales promotions, premiums, fund-raising, and educational needs. Special books or book excerpts also can be created to fit specific needs. For details, write Penguin Group (USA) Inc. Special Markets, 375 Hudson Street, New York, NY 10014.

Library of Congress Cataloging-in-Publication Data

Fraunfelder, Frederick T.
[Retirement Rx]
Retire right : the 8 scientifically proven traits you need for a happy, fulfilling retirement /
Frederick T. Fraunfelder, James H. Gilbaugh, Jr.
p.   cm.
Originally published: Retirement Rx. New York : Avery, © 2008
ISBN 978-1-58333-346-4
1. Retirement—United States.   2. Retirement—United States—Planning.   3. Baby boom generation—
United States.   I. Gilbaugh, James H.   II. Title.
HQ1063.2.U6F725   2009   2009009594
646.7'90973—dc22

Printed in the United States of America
1 3 5 7 9 10 8 6 4 2

BOOK DESIGN BY MEIGHAN CAVANAUGH

To our wives,

Yvonne and Marilyn,

Our families, our teachers, and our patients

ACKNOWLEDGMENTS

We have to acknowledge the game of golf! It was on the tee box of the ninth hole about six years ago that the moment of conception for our book took place. Dr. Fritz, aka "the planner," had taken a sabbatical from academic medicine. During that time he read everything he could on the nonfiscal side of retirement but wasn't satisfied with the information available to him. Dr. Jim, aka "the feeler," was semi-retired, thinking about his future and loaded with ideas on how he wanted to live it. We shared our thoughts with wives, families, and friends—thus the book was born.

Early thoughts and brainstorming were done with Charlie Allis, Bill Countant, Tom Cummins, Dick Cunningham, David Duxbury and Nancy Fletcher, Jack Faust, Joe Ferguson, Betty and John Gray, Britt Hayes, Jackie and Jerry Inskeep, Dan Isaak, Jack Johnston, Jan and Bob Kalina, Meritt Linn, Jim Maletis, Ruth and Joe Matarazzo, Ron Mehl, Courtland Mumford, Margaret Beth Neal, Frank O'Conner, Jim and Shirley Rippey, George Saslow, Alice Scannell, Gary Stewart, Fred and Pat Stickel, Ken Swan, Ann and Bill Swindell, Lou Terkla, Joan and Fred Thompson, and Ted Vigeland.

Early encouragement from Ken Blanchard, Eric Bollinger, Joe Hayes, Ed Pittock, and Betsy Vierck was important to us.

Many helped proof the book and came up with excellent suggestions, including Sigrid Button, Clem Connolly, Michael Gourley, Joanne Henry, Steve Kelley, Howard Lincoln, Patricia Robertson, Mollie Suits, Richard U'ren, and Werner Zeller.

The staff at the Casey Eye Institute at Oregon Health & Sciences University in Portland, Oregon gave support—Stephanie Lyons, Kelly Medlar, Nancy Mitchell, Joan Randall, Jeannine Ransome, Joe Robertson, Bree Vetsch, and Dave Wilson. We can't forget about our golf partners, who had to hear about, get quizzed, and have ideas bounced off them between erratic shots: Ernest Blatner, Dennis Dahlin, Al Henry, Fred Nomura, Dick Newman, and George Wells.

Our patients who gave their heartfelt time, talent, and ideas filling out lengthy questionnaires that became the basis of this book get extra credit. We owe "big-time" to Marilyn Gilbaugh, who is the voice of this book and made it what it is.

Our thanks to Jean Naggar and Mollie Glick of the Jean V. Naggar Literary Agency Inc., New York, our agents, for their guidance, suggestions, and help. To Karen Kelly for her amazing organizational skills. She truly was our book doctor. And to Lucia Watson of Avery, Penguin Group USA, New York, for her understanding and expertise.

CONTENTS

RETIRE RIGHT

INTRODUCTION: HURRY UP, YOUR LIFE IS WAITING

A s doctors with subspecialties in geriatrics, we have seen many patients on the brink of, just starting, or deeply into their retirement years. Their widely varied responses to this time and its challenges are remarkable. Some rise to new heights, whereas others seem ready to heave a heavy sigh, sag into a rocking chair, and settle in for good. For instance, one patient, Joanne, a recently retired real estate agent, told us her post–work life remained the same as it was while she was selling property. The only real difference was the gift of time that retirement had given her. She was now able to indulge in a midmorning haircut or spa treatment, linger over lunch, spend extra time browsing in the library or bookstore, or take her grandchildren or just herself to an afternoon matinee, all activities that she previously had time only for in the evening or on weekends. She considered this luxury truly golden.

When we compared Joanne's outlook to that of another patient, Brian, a man who had enjoyed a successful advertising career, we saw a dramatic difference. He could find little to enjoy about his retirement and went so far as to say that he had lost much of the pleasure of living! Even leisure activities that, as a working person, he had enjoyed participating in with his wife now held little interest for him, including dinner parties, cribbage competitions, or simply discussing current events with his spouse. Some of his withdrawal, Brian admitted, came from his increasing forgetfulness, which both scared and embarrassed him. But what bothered him most of all was spending so much time by himself—a situation he had rarely found himself in when he worked. Still, he lacked the will and the gumption to get out and get on with his life. He felt lost and without direction.

What makes one person embrace the second half of life, while another seems only capable of withdrawing from it? Why did some of our patients manage to maintain the vitality that had marked their working years while others failed to make the transition? We wanted to find some information about happy retirees that would assist our patients who were finding retirement a rough go. Exploring bookstores, libraries, and the Internet, we were relentless in our search for retirement advice. Most books we found focused on financial planning, and those that didn't were anecdotal—filled with standard recommendations to eat well, get enough sleep, and exercise. Good suggestions but too general and unscientific for our needs.

The search continued in our own practices: we began to look at our patients to identify with clinical certainty the skills, habits, and characteristics associated with people who experienced what we observed to be productive, well-adjusted, or "successful" retirements, which we define as richly endowed with good health, loving relationships, outside interests, and, most important, the resilience and wisdom to graciously accept the inevitable, which is loss—of family, friends, loved ones, health, memory, and, ultimately, life.

We wanted to collect accurate data, so we created and conducted a professionally designed survey. More than fifteen hundred of our patients were asked to anonymously fill out what we had come to call The Retirement Docs' Survey. It was the first time that a survey such as this had centered on retired people and their insights. The questionnaire consisted of multiple choice and essay questions, which took anywhere from an hour to an hour and a half to complete. The return rate was an unheard-of 72 percent. Our respondents replied candidly and often at length—their essays running the gamut from succinctly matter-of-fact to lengthy and deeply emotional, from warmly positive to grimly negative.

As you can imagine, we had amassed a tremendous amount of original research and strong data. We used well-established, controlled research and analysis methods to study the results, including assistance from a local university's gerontology statistics department. After our first look at what we had gathered, we realized that retirement success is not related to gender, marital status, children, hobbies, or grandchildren. Highly successful retirees come from all walks of life, from stay-at-home moms to corporate leaders, from astronauts to cab drivers, from people forced to retire because of office politics or poor health to those who couldn't walk away from the nine-to-five treadmill.

From the initial sorting, the statisticians identified four distinct phases of retirement, and nearly eighty traits that successful retirees shared. Those findings were then further distilled, which led us to identify eight specific traits that had the greatest statistical significance and were shared by all of the top 20 percent respondents in the Retirement Docs' Survey.

The four phases and the eight traits of highly successful retirees are the backbone of *Retirement Rx*. Helping you identify and use the traits you already possess and showing you how to develop those you may lack is the purpose of this book. It's the kind of "retirement investment" that pays dividends socially, intellectually, and physically.

PART ONE

■ ■ ■

PUTTING THE REST OF YOUR LIFE IN PERSPECTIVE

Part One of *Retirement Rx* makes the case for why you need to care about your retirement, and summarizes the findings of our research. You will also find a simplified and much shorter version of the original Retirement Docs' Survey, which we call the Retirement Docs' Quiz. Complete it and find out where you rank in terms of realizing your own successful retirement. Along with the quiz, we provide a customized prescription so that you can achieve or fine-tune any of the particular eight traits that we go into in detail in Part Two of *Retirement Rx*. Sharpen your pencils and let's get on with the rest of your life.

1

A New Kind of Retirement

Massive cultural change is about to happen. Older adults are poised to become trustees of civil life in America. As people live longer, healthier lives they are increasingly looking to give back to their communities and expand in new ways.

—Marc Freedman

Extended human longevity has rocked our world. In 1900, 4 percent of Americans were age sixty-five and older; 14 percent is the prediction for 2030. Currently, people eighty-five and older are the fastest-growing group in America. Consider this: In 1776 our life expectancy was just thirty-five years. In 1920 it had improved to where the healthiest among us could expect to live into our fifties. Today, we can look forward to living well into our seventies. If you are sixty and reading this, and free of heart disease or cancer, you could easily make it to your eighties or nineties. Medical breakthroughs and improvements in health care and lifestyle over the next two or three decades have led longevity forecasters to predict that men and women born in 2040 will have a general life expectancy of more than ninety!

More time on our hands means one thing: We better stop thinking of our post–employment life as an afterthought and start thinking of it as a second career—one that in all likelihood we'll spend as much if not more time involved in than our first! The reality is that we spend an average of twelve to sixteen years educating ourselves; twenty-five to forty years earning a living; and twenty-five to thirty-plus years in "retirement." If we play our

cards right, and we can, those two or three extra decades can be a time to explore and enjoy a new set of intellectual, cultural, social, and even romantic
possibilities.

We have a mutual friend named David. He is a with-it guy in his early
sixties who is in comparatively good health. It occurred to him one day that
after he left his job, he would have many remaining years to fill. He had to
change a long-held and conventional belief that one life equaled one career.
Both he and his wife, Nancy, who was nearing retirement, felt that their
"second career" would allow them to freely pick where they wanted to live,

Check out the time line below. Do you notice anything interesting about
it? These days, our retirement can easily equal and sometimes even sur-
pass our wage-earning years. This represents a tremendous paradigm
shift, one that changes the nature of retirement.

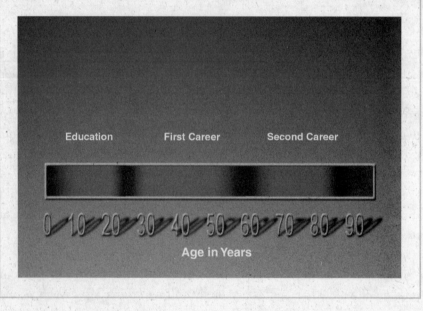

*Life can be divided into three ages: the age of learning, the age of working, and
the age of living.*

—RETIREMENT DOCS' SURVEY

what they wanted to do, and who they wanted to be and with whom. The couple moved, pursued hobbies they had no time for previously, and took up new interests. Nancy said she, very wisely in our opinion, saw retirement as a chance to do a life makeover.

THE FOUR PHASES OF RETIREMENT

Our survey data showed that retirement is divided into four distinct phases:

PHASE ONE: PLANNING FOR RETIREMENT

In this stage, you're fully employed but preparing and planning for life beyond your income-earning years. Ideally, fiscal planning should start in your thirties and at the latest in your early forties. By the time you reach your mid- to late-fifties, you should be financially prepared for your future. This is also the time to get serious about your vision for the nonfiscal side of retirement. Keep in mind that you should give yourself at least five to ten years *before* your semi- or full retirement to start laying the groundwork for a successful retirement. Phase one is a great time to "field-test" some leisure activities that you enjoy and that you can continue to pursue through the next three phases. Fifty-eight was the average age of our phase-one survey respondents.

PHASE TWO: SHIFTING INTO SEMIRETIREMENT

Semiretirement basically means that we are working part-time in some capacity and being paid for it. Statistically, we found that our respondents with high incomes and/or high levels of education spent more time in this phase than in phases three and four, probably because they derived a great deal of satisfaction from their jobs and were not ready to entirely give up their work. Many also enjoyed the extra income part-time work provided. Spending as much time as possible during phase two is good for your emotional, financial, and physical health—studies show that seniors who don't do any work at all die sooner than their peers who labor on.

You can stay in phase two for a very long time, in fact so long that you may spend just a few years, months, or even days in phases three and four. Think of all the well-known people who have managed this: At ninety-four, fitness guru and entrepreneur Jack LaLanne is still in phase two; Hollywood director Vincent Sherman, who died at ninety-nine in 2006, worked well into the 1980s as a TV director; the revered "French Chef," Julia Child, who lived to be ninety-two, started a television career at fifty-one and continued working well into her eighties. And there are many other examples of people who made their mark *after* they reached "retirement age."

The secrets to staying in phase two for a long time are, first, to maintain your health so you *can* work, and, second, to stay focused on work you truly *enjoy* and feel passionate about. Rid yourself of drudgery or any task that bores you. One of our favorite responses was from a guy who had been a podiatrist in his first career. He had decided "Enough of feet!" long before he left his full-time occupation behind. In his retirement, he found a part-time job driving a florist's delivery van. "Everybody loves getting flowers," he told us. With no complaints, and aromatic bouquets delighting him, he genuinely enjoyed his retirement's second career. Our phase-two survey respondents had an average age of sixty-seven.

Our fathers and grandfathers looked forward to a full retirement. For one thing, it indicated to their community that they had "earned it." They had worked hard and saved wisely. Since they were financially solvent, full retirement was an achievement of pride. The pendulum has swung. We no longer throw around the "when I retire" phrase. I look forward to being productive for as long as I can.

—RETIREMENT DOCS' SURVEY

PHASE THREE: FULL RETIREMENT

These are those carefree no-responsibility years you knew would be yours one day—you just might not have expected them to arrive so quickly. You might think that you can't wait to reach full retirement, but for many it's a tough transition. While there can be a thrill in not heading to work each morning, you may soon start to wonder what you are going to do with all the hours, days, and years yet to be lived.

Along with the challenges of having to fill free time, you may start to feel some health effects related to aging, or you may have new caregiving responsibilities for a mate or an aged parent. But the good news is that you can do more in this phase—from pursuing travel to learning a new language to engaging in artistic interests—with more vitality than ever before. The world is your oyster! Phase-three survey respondents had an average age of seventy-two.

> *I am afraid to retire. There, I wrote it and I'm reading it back to myself. I am afraid of retirement because I am my job. My friends are my friends because of my job. My life is framed around my job, and it's been that way for thirty-four years. I love what I do, I love my friends, and I love my job. I have a wife and a family and I cherish them, but they will be around and my job won't. My company is a small operation, and my wife and I work there together, not in the same office but in the same facility. In fact, that's how we met. So now I'll retire and my wife won't. I feel like a part of me is dying and in fact it is. I don't want a watch; I don't want a party. I don't want to leave my job. I don't want to be retired.*
>
> —RETIREMENT DOCS' SURVEY

PHASE FOUR: RESTRICTED FULL RETIREMENT

When you hit the last phase of retirement, you may experience many more limitations due to health, age, and finances. Without a doubt, the most difficult period of retirement is phase four. In this phase, adversity can come at you in waves, often with little or no time to recover between assaults. Loss of loved ones, depression, chronic disease, and aging changes all have an impact. We found that women weather this period better than men do, and in fact, a few of our female respondents felt that this was their happiest, most-successful phase. And as we've already explained, these days both men and women can expect to live into their eighties, nineties, and beyond, so it is crucial to learn how to deal with the last phase of retirement because chances are good that it will be a part of most of our lives. Some people die at their desks, but most of us won't. The average age of our phase-four survey respondents was seventy-eight.

THE RETIREMENT PHASES ARE DYNAMIC

The majority of us will experience many loops, twists, and turns throughout our retirement's four phases, until restrictions set in and physical and mental limitations makes it impossible for us to be as flexible. The really good news is that our society is fluid enough to find a place for the changing lives and needs of older adults. As our numbers increase, the world will—must—become more and more amenable to those needs.

Most of the people we studied worked full-time during phase one and then entered phase two's semiretirement by either cutting back on the hours they devoted to their jobs or by leaving a first career and starting another less-demanding or less time-consuming one that was either similar to their previous work or completely different (the accountant who opens a weekend-only antique shop, for example).

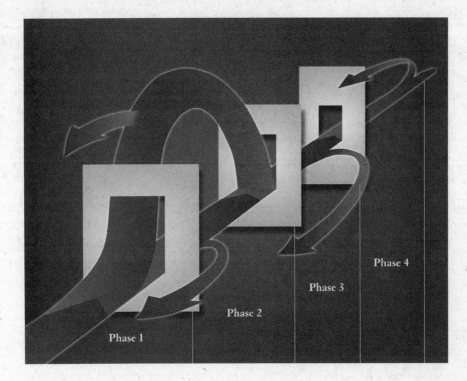

Phase 1

Phase 2

Phase 3

Phase 4

What is significant about the four phases is that they aren't necessarily progressive. Sometimes an opportunity comes along that won't take "no" for an answer, or a financial setback occurs, or just plain boredom sets in, and suddenly we go from phase two or three back to phase one's full employment. Or you may find yourself going directly from full employment right into phase three's full retirement. Then, just as suddenly, you find that you're back in phase two when you switch to a part-time job or engage in some paid consulting work.

Retirement success can also vary significantly between phases. For instance, many of our respondents reported that moving directly from full-time employment to full-time unemployment proved a most difficult adjustment. The majority of unhappy respondents were people who had been forced into mandatory and involuntary retirement owing to health issues, job loss, or an assortment of personal reasons. Retirement failure rates oc-curred most often in two areas: The first occurred among people who hopped directly from phase one's full-time employment into phase three's full-time unemployment. If you can transition into phase two's semiretirement and then taper off into a complete retirement, you're giving yourself an adjust-ment advantage. How long you spend tapering is highly individualized, so field-test various options before making life-changing decisions.

The second area of high failure rates arrives in phase four's restricted re-tirement. There is no doubt that phase four and the losses and life-altering changes it brings with it make the vast majority of us most vulnerable. But what was encouraging was that most people seemed able to get through the tough phases *if* they were able to make some attitude and behavior adjust-ments. Six to eighteen months after retirement most people become much more acclimated to their full retirement.

The Retirement Docs' Survey Says . . .

- 14 percent said retirement had changed their values and beliefs.
- 18 percent missed their old jobs.
- 21 percent had increased emotional problems related to aging.
- 20 percent experienced events that drastically affected their retirement plans.
- 20 percent were unhappy or were adjusting slowly to one or more of retirement's four phases.
- 26 percent thought retirement had changed their personalities.
- 30 percent needed considerable time to adapt. Some never fully ad-justed to retirement.
- 80 percent could bounce back after experiencing a major setback.

HIGHLY SUCCESSFUL RETIREES POSSESS THE SAME EIGHT TRAITS

Along with the four phases that emerged from our study came eight traits that every one of the most highly successful, well-adjusted, and content retirees shared (the top 20 percent of respondents). The good news is that even if you do not have all of these traits today, you can learn and master them, even if you think you have a genetic or cultural predisposition against them. What's more, possessing these eight traits *guarantees* you a highly successful retirement.

1. **Sowing Seeds—The Planner's Advantage**

   Of the eight traits, planning was statistically the most significant. Retirees who had a game plan for both the fiscal and the often-neglected nonfiscal aspects of retirement and who frequently revisited and updated that plan were the most satisfied with their lives during phases two, three, and four. Our most successful retirees were not primarily interested in money, but they had taken care of making sure they had enough of it to maintain their standard of living and sometimes even improve it.

2. **Accentuate the Positive—It's All About Attitude**

   Your *perception* of your own health, financial well-being, age, and achievements matters more to your retirement success than your *actual* age, health, income, or position in life. Social scientists and psychologists (Martin Seligman at the University of Pennsylvania being one of the most prominent) say that while people are genetically wired to be either cheerful or grouchy, all of us can learn to be more optimistic by examining how we think about situations and consciously changing negative thoughts into positive ones.

3. Go with the Flow—Accept Change

As we age, physical and mental challenges increase. For many of us, fear plays a huge role in adjusting to a new life without the titles, labels, or acknowledgments that life before retirement provided. Each advancing phase brings with it new trials and traumas. People with the ability to accept change in their first careers will almost always carry the same ability right into their second careers. Those who successfully overcome major upheavals before retirement usually have the confidence to tackle new challenges. In all four phases, the abilities to adapt and to accept change are crucial to your success.

Our highly successful retirees considered retirement their life's bonus and emphasized these advantages:

- Increased time devoted to leisure, social, and fitness-related activities.
- The ability to develop and enjoy a positive attitude toward life and aging.
- Involvement in meaningful and purpose-filled activities, including giving back to their society.
- Freedom to do what they like.
- The ability to live for the present, not for the past and not for the future. And many of them were doing so for the first time.
- A chance to spend more quality time with their mate or best friend.

---

4. A Little Help from Your Friends (and Family)

Develop a wide and varied support group. Surround yourself with people your age as well as those who are older and younger. Your intimate support group should include your spouse, life partner, or best friend; your children; grandchildren; and other extended family members. In this day and age, with the definition of "family" ever broadening, it can also include a larger community made up of close friends, religious and social organizations, special-interest groups, and, yes, even a pet. Ongoing involvement with your support-group family is one of those eight traits you must master throughout your four phases to guarantee a highly successful retirement.

5. Kick Back—Enjoy Your Leisure Time

Though the kinds of interests you pursue will often vary in each retirement phase, it's important to choose and develop a wide variety of both mentally and physically challenging activities in three specific categories: those you commonly do with one other person (playing chess, seeing a movie, romantic activities); those you do in a group (golf, cards, dinner parties); and those you do by yourself (reading a book, taking a walk, shopping). Some activities, for example, seeing a play or taking a vacation, can be done in any of these three variations. These are not necessarily things that you are passionate about, but they should be enjoyable activities that free your mind and relax you. They help reduce stress by unwinding your brain. That is the essence of leisure.

6. Here's to Your Health

Seventy-two percent of the people we surveyed considered heredity the prime factor for long-lasting health and a long life. *Not true.* After age sixty it's not your genetics but your lifestyle that is the main ingredient for longevity. Most serious hereditary diseases expose themselves before age sixty; after sixty, it's not so much the hand you've been dealt as how you play it. Highly successful retirees take care of themselves: They have regular medical checkups, watch their diets, follow exercise programs, don't smoke, watch their alcohol intake, and control their weight. People with planned exercise programs had up to almost 70 percent less physical disability in the final year of their lives: yes, year is singular and it says 70 percent! That's quite a final bonus if we can learn to take care of ourselves.

7. Passion and a Purpose

In retirement, your identity no longer comes from a job title but from an overall view of yourself. The earlier you figure out what gives you a sense of fulfillment, the more successful you'll make your retirement. Engaging in an activity that makes time fly, an activity so intriguing or meaningful that you get lost in it, is a passion to hang on to. Stamp collecting, gardening, antiquing, training for and running a marathon, writing a screenplay, playing a musical instrument, and volunteering for a political or social cause are all examples of engaging and purposeful passions. And don't be afraid to make a mistake in the process of developing a new passion; they can be great learning tools. You have time to try a variety of activities and find those you really love.

8. Let the Spirit Move You

In retirement, having a belief in something "bigger" than we are can offer a major assist when we're faced with trauma. This is especially important in phases three and four, when setbacks occur more frequently, such as deteriorating physical and emotional health (in ourselves or a partner); the death of a partner, family member, or close friend; increased caregiving responsibilities; and/or major illness. Many of our respondents told us that spirituality offers them strength, solace, and hope. It's clear that facing the last stages of life without some form of spirituality is an enormous challenge.

There's a caveat to these eight traits: The 80 percent of respondents who did not make the highly successful mark (we've dubbed them the Not Yet Such Successful Retirees) lacked one or more of the eight traits. We found that every survey respondent who was missing *even one* was unable to meet the highly successful criteria. The same survey information also pinpointed that failure in, or omission of, any of the eight traits often caused failure within one or more of the four phases. That tells us that you can have all eight traits working for you in one phase, but if you fail at any one of them in another phase, you're not where you should be, and the warranty on our guarantee will run out.

We also noticed that the importance and weight of each trait varies depending on the phase, even though, for success, they are all required to one degree or another for every phase. For example, spirituality does not seem to be as important during phases one through three as it is in phase four, when it becomes crucial. Likewise, the ability to actively accept change is essential for success in phases one through three, but it becomes somewhat muted during phase four, when much of the change, except for the "final passage" may have already taken place in your life. As you read about the traits in-depth in part two, you will learn more about how and why the intensity of each trait changes throughout your life.

SO WHEN DO YOU KNOW YOU SHOULD RETIRE?

There is no best or set time to retire. While it is usually an individual decision, sometimes, as we said earlier, retirement from a job can be forced upon people by circumstances beyond their control. If it is possible to take a sabbatical from your job (many companies actually offer this benefit), do so as a way of field-testing retirement. Or take all the vacation time you can in one fell swoop. If you hate it, well, keep working. If you loved lengthy time off, consider these guidelines as a way of helping you determine whether it is time to call it quits on your first career and get going on your second:

- **Take a Serious Look at Your Financial Fitness:** If you can't maintain your preretirement standard of living, don't retire, or consider working part-time. Our data and the data of others suggest that not being able to live in the style to which you are accustomed is a significant factor of unhappiness for retirees.
- **Location, Location, Location:** Happiness in retirement depends, for many of us, on one's ability to be in an environment in which

we feel happy and in control. If you are fiscally fit and live in a place or can move to a place that you love, you're ready to roll.

■ **Go with Your Gut:** People know much more about themselves than they give themselves credit for. Take some quiet time and think about what you really want and what you are ready for. Most of us know when it's time to go into phase two or three, if we give it some serious thought. Make an appointment with yourself to think about your overall feelings about retirement, your health, your mate, your marriage or relationship, and whether you still like your job. These factors should also be taken into account before you make the decision to go from "business as usual" to no work at all.

ASSESS YOUR RETIREMENT READINESS

To further explore when and if it's time for you to retire and feel good doing so, ask yourself the following questions and then answer them using a scale of one to five:

1. Strongly disagree; 2. Disagree; 3. I'm neutral; 4. Agree; and 5. Strongly agree.

I have a gut feeling that it's time for me to slow down or quit work. _____

Only a small part of my self-worth comes from my work. _____

Generally, leisure time gives me more satisfaction than my work. _____

Most of my social life revolves around people outside of my work. _____

I don't have as strong a work ethic as I once did. _____

Financially I can maintain my standard of living if I don't work.   _____

I look at retirement as a newfound freedom and a rebirth,
not an ending.   _____

I have multiple interests outside of my work and have taken time
to develop leisure activities.   _____

If I take time away from work, it does not cause me or my mate
stress.   _____

I don't want a structured, routine life.   _____

I look at retirement as a time to further explore happiness.   _____

I have things in place that can fill the void both in time and the
self-image that my work provided.   _____

Your Total Score: _____

Scoring:
48–60   You are ready to retire.
36–47   Consider semiretirement.
35 and under   Start planning before you stop working.

Now that you have a feel for when you should retire, it's time to turn your attention to what your chances are at this moment to be successful at retirement. Even if you don't have all the traits of a highly successful retiree now, you can work on developing them.

2

THE RETIREMENT
DOCS' QUIZ

Happy families are all alike, but each unhappy family is unhappy in its own way.

—*ANNA KARENINA*, LEO TOLSTOY

Likewise,

Highly successful retirees are all alike, but each unhappy retiree is unsuccessful in his or her own way.

—RETIREMENT DOCS' SURVEY

If you're flipping through *Retirement Rx* and happen upon this page, STOP! Doing so could revolutionize your approach to your retirement. Give us ten minutes of your time and we'll give you back some information that will serve you well for the rest of your life. We have condensed the original survey questions from our large survey and created this more-streamlined version, the Retirement Docs' Quiz. Taking it is your big first step in guaranteeing a highly successful retirement. Your quiz results will accurately predict how well you can expect to do through all four phases of retirement. Even if you're already retired, the quiz will help you identify which areas you need to work on to improve and embrace the rest of your retirement. It's never too late to make changes.

The grading system results are accurate. In fact, in scientific lingo, our data have an alpha coefficient (reliability) of 0.75, and are highly predictive and acceptable for publication in peer-reviewed scientific journals. It's a real barometer, pointing to the kind of success you can expect from your retirement. You'll discover whether you need a tune-up in one or more of the eight traits. If you do, that's okay! Most of us do. Better to know now so that you can prepare yourself and get to work. The quiz will help you identify exactly where and/or what you're lacking. In part two we look at each trait in-depth and offer a prescription for developing and improving each one, if you find that you need work in one or more.

In order to get the most out of your retirement, retake the quiz whenever you enter or are about to enter a new phase. Each phase may require a different combination of skills and strengths, which often vary with the passage of time. Circle your response to each of the following questions, then enter that number in the "My Score" box in the column on the far right. After you've completed the quiz, total your score at the bottom. We recommend that you take this quiz whenever you have a major change in your life (use different-colored pencils so that you can note your progress over time). *Please* be honest in your answers! If you're not, we can't help you. You're only hurting yourself if you are not completely candid.

PLEASE RATE YOURSELF ON THE FOLLOWING:	POOR	FAIR	GOOD	VERY GOOD	EXCELLENT	MY SCORE
1. I can adapt or be flexible when events or circumstances in my life change.	0	2.5	5	7.5	10	

PLEASE RATE YOURSELF ON THE FOLLOWING:	POOR	FAIR	GOOD	VERY GOOD	EXCELLENT	MY SCORE
2. I am satisfied with the social support from my family and friends.	0	2.5	5	7.5	10	
3. I am satisfied with my financial planning for retirement.	0	2.5	5	7.5	10	
4. I am satisfied with my planning for the nonfinancial aspects of retirement.	0	2.5	5	7.5	10	
5. I will be able to maintain my standard of living after retirement.	0	2.5	5	7.5	10	
6. I have a positive mental outlook.	0	2.5	5	7.5	10	
7. I make an effort to control my weight.	0	2.5	5	7.5	10	

PLEASE RATE YOURSELF ON THE FOLLOWING:	POOR	FAIR	GOOD	VERY GOOD	EXCELLENT	MY SCORE
8. I have annual medical checkups.	0	2.5	5	7.5	10	
9. I am satisfied with my general health.	0	2.5	5	7.5	10	
10. Religion or spirituality positively influences my life.	0	2.5	5	7.5	10	
11. I have enough intellectual stimulation.	0	2.5	5	7.5	10	
12. I engage in and enjoy enough social and leisure activities.	0	2.5	5	7.5	10	
13. I am satisfied with my sex life.	0	2.5	5	7.5	10	
14. I get regular exercise and physical activity.	0	2.5	5	7.5	10	
15. I have a passion for multiple projects and/or subjects.	0	2.5	5	7.5	10	

PLEASE RATE YOURSELF ON THE FOLLOWING:	POOR	FAIR	GOOD	VERY GOOD	EXCELLENT	MY SCORE
16. I am involved in activities that make society better.	0	2.5	5	7.5	10	
17. I am satisfied with the variety in my leisure activities.	0	2.5	5	7.5	10	
18. I am happy with my life.	0	2.5	5	7.5	10	
19. I see myself as lucky or fortunate.	0	2.5	5	7.5	10	
20. Education level	Less than high school 0	High school 2.5	Some college 5	College degree 7.5	Postgraduate work or degree 10	
21. I smoke.	>1 pack 0	>½ pack 2.5	<½ pack 5	Quit 7.5	Never 10	
22. Alcohol consumption 1 drink = 12-oz. beer, 5-oz. wine, or 1.5-oz. liquor	>21 drinks/ week 0	14–21 drinks/ week 2.5	<14 drinks/ week 5	<7 drinks/ week 7.5	None/ occasionally 10	

Your Total Score: _____

Your Score and What It Means to You

IF YOU SCORED BETWEEN 185 AND 220:

Congratulations. You're with the top 20 percent of our Retirement Docs' Survey's respondents, our Highly Successful Retirees. Continue fine-tuning specific traits, particularly as you enter each new phase. You can guarantee yourself your own highly successful retirement if you maintain these eight traits.

IF YOU SCORED BETWEEN 150 AND 184:

Your score is in the top 40 percent, indicating that you're well on your way to a highly successful retirement but need some fine-tuning in specific traits. Which areas were you lacking in? For example, if you gave low scores to health-related questions (for example, you don't exercise), you will need to pay more attention to the health trait chapter. If you gave social questions low scores (for example, your circle of friends is very small), you need to pay attention to the support group, leisure activity, passions and purpose, and spirituality trait chapters.

IF YOU SCORED BETWEEN 120 AND 149:

Your score is in the middle of the pack, the average. Your future may be promising, but currently it's far from highly successful. You really need to focus on specific traits. Create a list of them *and make a conscious effort to improve them on a daily basis*. Mindfulness is really the key because you are so close to achieving a highly successful retirement. With a little effort and by paying close attention to the information provided for you in the following chapters, you can retake the test in six months and see a change for the better in your score.

IF YOU SCORED BETWEEN 85 AND 119:

Well, the bad news is that you've got lots of work to do. But the good news is that it is work you'll enjoy because it's all about you and your success. Your score is in the lowest 40 percent, so it's best to recognize and concentrate on the areas that indicate a need for additional attention. Whatever the phase, don't put it off: Get to work on those changes *now*. If you're not retired, commit to spending significant amounts of time working on the eight traits on your own, with a spouse or friend, or with a professional. You *can* become a highly successful retiree.

IF YOUR SCORE IS 84 OR LOWER:

It is definitely time to dig in. Your score falls in the lowest 20 percent of the Retirement Docs' Survey respondents. There is hope, especially since you've taken the time to pick up this book and take the quiz. We all have a chance to enjoy and benefit from retirement. Do a lot of checking back with *Retirement Rx* trait chapter guidelines, and retake the quiz while tracking when you change phases or when something major happens in your life.

No matter where you are on the scorecard, please take time to read about each trait more in-depth. For those who have work to do, start by setting small goals and following the advice at the end of each of the following trait sections.

PART TWO

A HIGHLY SUCCESSFUL RETIREMENT AND HOW TO MAKE IT YOUR OWN

The chapters in this section examine each of the important traits that make up all highly successful retirements. If you did well in a trait, meaning that you have a high score, don't neglect to read its corresponding chapter, as it will provide you with insights and ideas on how to maintain your strength in that area. If you are weak in one or more areas, then please pay special attention to the chapters that cover them for ideas on how to empower yourself and increase your chances of a highly successful retirement. Every trait chapter includes:

- a description and explanation of each trait.
- data and real-life anecdotes particular to the trait from the Retirement Docs' Survey and other individuals.
- the latest pertinent scientific research.
- a diagnosis so you can tell where you stand in terms of each trait.
- a prescription, including short- and long-term fine-tuning, to help you develop that trait more fully.

3

Trait One: Sowing Seeds—The Planner's Advantage

Someone to love, something to do,
and something to look forward to.
—Ancient Chinese Proverb

Highly successful retirees ranked planning as far and away the most important trait for achieving a positive retirement. Interestingly, nonfiscal planning slightly edged out the fiscal—it's not all about the money after all! It's not too much of a surprise because most of us intuitively know that in order to have a successful retirement we need to feel safe and secure. That's why many of us, very wisely, start planning for the fiscal side of retirement ahead of time, while still working full-time. Few people believe that a Social Security check alone will be sufficient for their needs. Our survey also revealed that while 92 percent of our respondents had done some financial retirement planning, only a third of them told us they'd given little to no thought to nonfiscal plans.

Transitioning from work to retirement is one of the hardest things I've ever done.
For me, the key to doing it successfully is ongoing planning.
—Retirement Docs' Survey

Like a savvy entrepreneur, you've got to do your research and develop a solid, realistic "business plan" when you are preparing for a second career. If you don't know how you'll spend your time, you won't enjoy a strong quality of life, and it doesn't really matter how many dollars you have in the bank. Highly successful retirees didn't scramble to put plans together weeks before they left their jobs. They started early, thinking, researching, and laying groundwork. The good news is that if you're reading this book, you've probably realized that you need to start planning for retirement. Even if you're already retired, the information in this book can help you enjoy retirement even more.

There are six categories that must be addressed if you hope to plan a highly successful retirement:

- Your finances
- Your work
- Your life with your mate
- Your professional and/or personal-growth goals
- Your sense of identity
- Your leisure time

As you work through the questions and ideas in this chapter, bear in mind that it's okay to approach planning in your own way. Maybe you're a person who likes to analyze data, making lists of the pros and cons of each decision you make; maybe you prefer thoughtful meditation or brainstorming with your friends; or maybe you'd rather register for a class. The questions we pose here will help you organize your thoughts. It doesn't matter how you come up with your retirement plan, just as long as you spend time making one. Speaking of spending time, be sure you spend some of it looking through our Retirement Resources at the back of the book for classes, support groups, and fields of study that are ready and waiting to assist you.

FINANCIAL SECURITY

Two-thirds of my retired clients who started to plan for retirement after age forty said that they should have started much sooner.

—RETIREMENT DOCS' SURVEY

It doesn't take a Wharton degree to know that the earlier you start formulating a financial plan for your retirement, the better. Our survey results revealed that the key to success isn't the total amount of assets accumulated—it's the ability to maintain your standard of living throughout the four phases. Ideally, you want to start setting some money aside in your late thirties or early forties. As doctors, we know when to refer out, and we'll leave specific investment advice up to the personal-finance experts.

A professional personal-finance manager will be able to help you determine whether you need to work during phase two, and how much money you need to make in order to fund phases three and four. As you begin to plan for the financial side of retirement, consider how soon you plan to retire, whether you will continue to pursue some paid work once you do scale back, and whether downsizing to a smaller, easier-to-maintain, and more conveniently located (to stores, entertainment, etc.) house makes sense for you. Retirees also should make contingency plans for the unforeseen complications of getting older, including illness and disabilities.

One potentially costly aspect of an active retirement, involving various leisure pursuits and travel, along with typical health-care and home maintenance costs, is an increase in spending—think sport activity fees; theater tickets; plane fare to faraway destinations; meals in restaurants; indulging in interests such as wine, rare books, antiques, or other collectible items; doctor visits; and home maintenance costs (as you get older, you often have to pay someone else to clean, maintain, and make basic home repairs). Almost all the respondents who indicated that they'd given some thought to their financial security ahead of time were able to cover the costs of their retirement.

If you have fiscal plans in place for retirement—a 401(k), pension, IRA, or savings account that you contribute to regularly, a diversified portfolio of stocks and bonds, and/or real estate investments, for example—you will likely be in the same position as our highly successful retirees find themselves: 65 percent of them indicated that their postretirement income remained the same as their preretirement income, 29 percent said it increased after retirement, and only 6 percent reported that it declined. Those who experienced a voluntary decrease in their income but kept their standard of living similar to what they had enjoyed in their working years fared well. However, those who experienced a forced or involuntary decrease in their standard of living felt significant stress and unhappiness.

Ask yourself the following two questions about financial planning. Your answers should help you and your financial planner get started on the appropriate strategy for your circumstance:

1. Do you project that you can maintain your current standard of living after you stop working full-time?
   - I believe that I am on the right track to maintaining my current standard of living in my retirement.
   - I don't know whether I can maintain my current standard of living when I am retired.
   - I don't think I will be able to maintain my current standard of living in my retirement.

2. If not, then have you thought about how to reduce spending (say, by cutting back or rearranging costs of social outings, reducing gift giving, or moving from a house you own to a smaller, less costly one or even a rental) so that you can maintain financial security and the freedom to pursue the activities that you love?
   - Some things that can reduce my spending when I am retired are:
     a.
     b.
     c.
     d.
     e.

NONFISCAL SECURITY

The difference between the moderately successful and the highly successful retirees in our survey was the amount of time and energy highly successful respondents devoted to nonfiscal planning. One of the most interesting findings of our study is that once you meet a certain threshold of financial security, your happiness in retirement isn't determined by how much money you have to spend—it's determined by how fulfilling you find post-retirement work, relationships, well-being, and hobbies.

WORK

Postretirement work is certainly part of a larger financial picture, but we think it is more important to your emotional, psychological, and physical well-being than it is to your pocketbook. We discovered that the longer you work, the longer and happier your life will be. That's why we listed it first under nonfinancial retirement planning.

AARP's latest survey reports that 80 percent of Baby Boomers plan to do some work after retirement. Although most of us will stay in the same occupation, many of us will branch out or start businesses unrelated to our previous occupation, which may provide another bonus, retraining or education. And don't think it will be difficult for you to find a job once you've hit sixty or seventy. Depending on where you live and what you want to do, you may find employment riches waiting for you. Many economists predict that by 2030, the United States could experience a labor shortage of 35 million workers. Many businesses have responded to what they see as a coming labor crisis by seeking out older workers. There are also advantages for these companies in hiring older workers: Insurance costs are lower, since many senior citizens are enlisted in government health-care programs; older workers are more experienced and reliable than their younger counterparts; and senior citizens are a growing population that represents a large block of available and willing labor.

Consider the following factors when thinking about the kind and amount of work you want to do in your second career. Your answers will help you pinpoint the best job options for you:

- Why are you working?
- Do you work *primarily* for the income or for the activity?
- How much money do you have to make? Would there be a job you would not take because the pay was too little?
- What values, personality traits, and strengths influenced your choice of a first career? Have these values, traits and strengths changed over time? If so, what kinds of jobs would make best use of your current attributes?
- How much did your first career contribute to your sense of self or identity? Were there parts of your personality left untapped by your first career? If so, what kinds of jobs would allow you to explore these other aspects of yourself?
- Do you want to stay in your field? Would your current employer consider keeping you on part-time or as a consultant? Have you discussed this possibility with your company?
- Do you want to do something different?
- Do you want to reserve more recreational time during your active retirement years? How will this affect the kind of work you choose?
- How introverted or extroverted are you, and what level of social interaction would you like your second career to provide?
- Would a job that puts you in contact with people, such as part-time retail or restaurant work, or a customer-service role, be appealing, or would a more autonomous position that gives you a chance to learn new skills hold more interest (such as computer programming)?
- Is there a business you always wanted to start that uses your skills, talents, or interests—such as a book or antique store, craft, or carpentry? If so, how much capital would you need? Would you have to get a small-business loan? Is there a location near you that could

support such an enterprise, or could you combine the start of the business with a move to a location where you want to put down new roots?

■ How many hours a week do you plan to work?

■ Do you plan to work the same number of hours for the indefinite future, or do you plan to scale back further in the next few years?

Planning With Your Mate

Planning your second career is about you, but if you've got a life partner, then you won't be successful in putting your plans into action unless you consider your partner. Like a starry-eyed youth embarking on marriage for the first time, we've known newly retiring couples who imagine that their "new" life together will be blue skies, long walks hand in hand, sharing sunsets, and rekindling their early romance. Lovely, wonderful, and most certainly possible, but remember, we're living real life here. Retirement usually brings with it more "for better and for worse," and we all agree that life together is best when it's "for better."

When discussing your mutual retirement plans, talk about the lifestyle you'd both like to lead, where you both want to live, and who you both want to be close to. You may find that your visions differ on some or even many aspects of retirement. Think compromise. Settle on a plan that works for both of you. For example, you may have to put your dreams of living on a golf course in the sun on hold until your spouse is ready to retire and/or thinking the same way. If your lifelong ambition is to climb in the Himalayas and your mate hates heights, talk about climbing with a group of friends while your spouse realizes a life's dream doing what's high on his or her list. Retirement doesn't equal communal house arrest. You don't have to and you shouldn't do everything together. Chances are good that you haven't lived joined at the hip before retirement. Remember that a healthy relationship is built on independence and mutual respect, plus your togetherness.

(continued)

How much "together" time do you envision having on a daily basis? This is especially important if you both worked full-time in different businesses. Reducing work schedules or entirely eliminating them, then adjusting to a lack of structure, can be a shock to both of your emotional systems. "Who is this person?" you might ask yourself, if you spend an entire week at home with your spouse. If you find yourself irritated with a mate who is now home full-time, don't let your frustration fester—address your concerns and feelings honestly, compassionately, and right away. Figure out a way for each of you to spend time apart during the day—even if it is in separate rooms.

A retired couple we know, Sally and Ralph, prepared for constant togetherness by staying involved in their community. They downsized and bought a smaller house just a few blocks away from the one in the same town where they raised their family. They love riding bikes in the country, and three of their four children (and their offspring) live within fifty miles, so they visit them very often, alone or together. They have a variety of friends nearby as well. Ralph is involved in the local Rotary Club, and Sally is president of her town's garden club. In short, they have strong ties to the community. All of these social ties help alleviate any potential tension they may have when they find themselves at home, together, all the time. When they want to get away or really need a change of scenery, the couple can, together or individually, visit their fourth son, who lives with his wife and son about 120 miles away. And yes, their son and his family look forward to those visits.

PERSONAL GROWTH AND SELF-ESTEEM

How do you want to be remembered? And how are you going to become that person? Many of us found our sense of identity and self-esteem in our first careers—whether we were involved in a successful occupation or supervised a successful household and family or both. If you're one of these people, where is your new self-image going to come from in retirement? For some of us, this might be an opportunity to reinvent our identities and leave a different or bigger legacy. Maybe you've worked in a corporate office and you're ready to give back to your community through volunteer work or by organizing or sponsoring a social interest group. Or maybe you want to mentor young people or someone starting out in your business. Perhaps you simply want to spend more time with family and friends because there was limited time with them while you were working. Whatever you decide is important, however, plan for your legacy not just in terms of leaving your money to a good cause. Your time and involvement while you're still around are just as important.

Your interests and skills will be best used in volunteer work that actually means something to you. If you're an animal lover, you could find yourself happier than you ever imagined working with those furry wonders—and it's on your own schedule. If you love art, becoming a docent at a museum or a member of a development committee are both wonderful ways to spend your time, are legacy-building, and help establish a solid and ongoing social structure.

Ann, one of our survey respondents, wrote that with just two and a half years left before she would retire at age sixty-five, she was busy planting the seeds for her happily anticipated free time and her legacy—literally. While Ann and her husband are still working, they use vacation time to visit successful community-garden projects all across the United States. Then, when retirement arrives, the first thing Ann plans to do, she told us, is to throw her own retirement party and invite all the people in her neighborhood to be her guests. Providing plenty of food and drink, she will conclude the celebration with a presentation on how she imagines the evolving community garden in her own area becoming even larger and more lush, with recommendations on how to involve people of all ages in its expansion and continuation.

Both of us know Bill, a man in his seventies, who has been married, divorced, and remarried. As a result, he has raised a combined family. Bill is accumulating grandchildren faster than he had ever anticipated. He has always been keenly interested in woodworking, and found that making a set of building blocks each from a different wood, for each grandchild's third birthday, held ongoing educational benefits for both his grandchildren and himself. In the process, Bill has become a recognized expert on woods both common and rare. His love of his grandchildren and his woodworking provides him with a positive self-image, a creative outlet (each set of blocks has a unique style of lettering and different images), and continuing family and community involvement.

Here are some questions that will help you identify your second career self-image and legacy-building aspirations, whether they be recognition from a world body, getting yourself a new body, or enjoying, for the first time, being more of a homebody. As you see it:

- How do you want to be remembered? What can you do to make it happen?
- What is a pressing matter facing society today? How can you address that need?
- What are the charities or interest groups or political candidates you have contributed to in the past, and which ones do you contribute time or money to now? Do any of them need the skills you can provide?
- Can any of your passions or interests be matched with a cause or nonprofit institution?

LEISURE

Research has shown that the leisure activities people pursue when they retire are the same as or similar to the ones they pursued before retirement. For instance, people who liked to do things in groups are not all of a sudden going to enjoy solo activities, and vice versa. However, this does *not* mean that you can engage only in activities you've enjoyed in the past. Far from it. It does mean that your essential self needs to be reflected in the activities you pursue. For instance, a person who has always loved reading cookbooks and cooking before retirement may now pursue cooking lessons, expanding techniques and in-depth knowledge of different cuisines with the possibility of combining travel, cultural study, and cuisine.

A soon-to-be-retired attorney we know, Mike, will combine his interest in certain leisure activities and personal passions with a plan to be close to his favorite niece, her husband, and their children, who live in Manhattan. Since he is long-divorced, single, and has no children, being close to Amanda and her family is important. But so is his love of people watching, walking, opera, music, and theater. Still living in New Jersey, he's already bought a seven-hundred-square-foot apartment in the city, which he sublets for the time being—the profit on rent he gets each month goes right into his "opera fund." The smaller place will be the perfect size for him when he stops working.

Enjoying a variety of leisure activities is actually one of the eight traits of all highly successful retirees. We've devoted an entire section to it (see page 17) so we won't spend too much time in this chapter going into it in great depth. However, here are a few questions to get you thinking and planning future leisure pursuits:

- What parts of retirement are you most excited about?
- How do you plan to realize these goals? Are you finally going to write that novel or perfect your golf swing, spend more time with grandkids or devote your time to a good cause?
- Can you make a list of six of your current leisure activities, and try to pinpoint which of them you'd like to devote more time to?
  1.
  2.
  3.
  4.
  5.
  6.

THE DIAGNOSIS

In first careers, we each have our individual styles. Some people like dead-lines and structure, whereas others are procrastinators or prefer to fly by the seat of their pants. We're likely to approach our second careers similarly. There are many different ways to plan for retirement. For example, Dr. Fritz is an organized, deadline-oriented person. He started planning for the nonfiscal side of retirement way ahead of time.

> *My father, who lived to be ninety-four, was miserable in retirement. He was in show business, and when he left the stage, he had nothing to replace it. I witnessed his unhappiness and I didn't want it to happen to me.*
>
> *Ten years before my projected retirement I took a sabbatical, and I read everything I could get my hands on and talked to anyone and everyone who knew anything about retirement. I then formulated my nonfiscal plan by field-testing various leisure activities. I took up golf for the first time at age fifty-five. I field-tested the art of bonsai but gave it up because my wife and I traveled a lot, and caring for the trees became stressful. I have always been a "planning kind of guy" and became obsessed with how to become highly successful in retirement.*
>
> —DR. FRITZ

In contrast, Dr. Jim is more spontaneous and intuitive. His retirement plan is likewise more spontaneous, but he has still laid the groundwork for a secure retirement.

> *My life has been patterned after what I learned from my extended family. I'm lucky enough to have lots of relatives, including down-and-outers and multi-millionaires. Observing my family provided examples for me throughout my life. I saw firsthand that "the almighty dollar" was not my answer for living a successful life. Whatever my life's goals demanded, I always made time for leisure activities.*
>
> *Early in my career I made a financial retirement plan but never thought about the need to plan for the nonfiscal. Along with a very full and satisfying ca-*

reer, I maintained a wide social network and multiple hobbies. My wife calls me
an emotional planner. Researching the materials for this book, mainly creating
the Retirement Docs' Survey, and working with the data it provided has me fas-
cinated with the knowledge that eight traits can guarantee my own successful re-
tirement. If ever a doctor got a taste of his own medicine, this is it!

—DR. JIM

Whatever your style, the following questions should help you determine
the planning you have ahead of you to ensure your successful retirement,
and how much work it will entail.

1. What amount of time have you devoted to planning the nonfiscal side
   of retirement?
   ■ I have given as much time to the nonfiscal as to the fiscal.
   ■ I have spent some time planning for the nonfiscal aspects of
     my retirement.
   ■ I have given the nonfiscal little to no thought.

2. Have you talked with your mate about your retirement plans and
   mutual interests regarding retirement?
   ■ Yes.
   ■ No.

3. Have you investigated postretirement work options?
   ■ Yes.
   ■ No.
   List five that you are involved with now and/or would like to continue or explore when you're retired.
   a.
   b.
   c.
   d.
   e.

4. Have you found any activities that will allow you to contribute to your family or society, providing you with the same sense of fulfillment that your first career gave you?
   ■ Yes.
   ■ No.

5. Have you started pursuing a few more leisure activities—activities that specifically stimulate your mind—so that you'll have other interests should physical limitations dictate? Think about what is of interest to you—and remember, none of it is set in stone.
   ■ Yes.
   ■ I've given some thought to them.
   ■ No.
   List five that might be of interest to you now—remember, these can change and should be updated at least once a year. Change is good!
   a.
   b.
   c.
   d.
   e.

If you answered the preceding questions with positive responses and had no problems filling in the lists, you are a planner and on the right track to realizing a fulfilling retirement. If some of your answers or lack of them indicate that you have not given the time needed to ensure a successful head start, it's essential that you start focusing on the areas that need attention. When completed, it will put you on a par with our top 20 percent. We can guarantee you that your plans will prove to be an asset to you for the rest of your life.

THE RETIREMENT DOCS' PRESCRIPTION

Whatever your current phase of retirement, it's time to start transitioning from "making a living" to "making your life"—a great slogan for a T-shirt! Now is the time to start thinking about where you want to live; who you want to spend time with; how you want to spend your time; and, most important, who *you* want to be. If you're not naturally a planner, this might sound daunting, but it needn't be. You've taken the first steps by picking up this book, taking the retirement quiz, and pinpointing which of the eight traits you need to develop further. Now please continue reading about the other seven traits, and you'll find yourself well on your way to a fantastic rest of your life!

4

TRAIT TWO: ACCENTUATE THE POSITIVE—IT'S ALL ABOUT ATTITUDE

Any fact facing us is not as important as our attitude towards it,
for that determines our success or failure.

—NORMAN VINCENT PEALE

There is a subgroup within our highly successful retirees who are in poor physical health, but, because of strong positive attitudes along with their ability to accept change (and often a strong spirituality as well), they cope with any disabilities exceedingly well. In fact, our perception of our health or our attitude toward it seems to be as important as our actual health. For example, we know a guy named George, who is being treated for prostate cancer. Instead of wallowing in self-pity and viewing his diagnosis as a death sentence, he is treating his disease as an opportunity. He has started a sixty-plus support group at the hospital where he gets his chemo; he volunteers as a peer counselor to men who have just been diagnosed; and once a month he reads stories to the kids in the children's wing of the hospital. The caring obligations George has established may well make him live longer, and they will without a doubt give him a better mental quality of life.

It goes without saying that George will encounter some tough times, but by and large his optimistic behavior will get him through it.

Then there's Shirley—the arthritis in her shoulders and knees causes her pain a good deal of the time. You'd never know it, though. She's too busy knitting sweaters and blankets for her newest grandson, finding interesting yarns to use, and searching out novelty or vintage buttons to embellish them. So taken has the woman in the knitting store become with Shirley's efforts, she wants her to make some of her creations to sell in the shop! Who has time to "feel the pain" when there's so much to do?

A good attitude is not just of aid to those who are sick. Our friend Phillip has a ball throwing huge parties. He's never ruffled if the band arrives late or if the red wine doesn't show. Indeed, Phillip has an innate ability to turn negatives into positives, which we attribute to his flexible nature. Phillip just isn't rigid and certainly isn't into perfection. He innately knows that parties are supposed to be fun. He knows that the band *will* eventually turn up, and he's got enough cranberry juice for anybody desperate for something red to drink, which he labels Phillip's Folly, Vintage 2007, which will in the end make his party even more memorable.

Likewise, one of our wives works on call with her friend, Suzanne, who founded and runs a home-based company that creates and organizes indexes for books. Publishing companies often outsource indexing, and this fifty-something dynamo has all the work she can handle; yet she appears to remain minimally stressed as a project's deadline approaches. Nineteenth-century British statesman Benjamin Disraeli once said, "The secret of success is constancy to purpose." We suspect that that is just what is happening in Suzanne's case: She is positive that her projects will get done because she never lets a job overwhelm her. She calmly takes each aspect of indexing step-by-step, bit by bit, and her projects are always completed on schedule.

Eloise is a gracious grandmother of eleven. She is one of those timeless beauties, and although we would never ask her age, we guess her to be somewhere in her late seventies. She has an unflappable ability to have all of her grandchildren running around her house, if not actually hanging off her, as she throws open the doors of her home to a fund-raising event benefiting one of the many organizations with which she is involved. There she stands, greeting well over one hundred guests with ease and heartfelt warmth, with no attempt to rid herself of the children. She is so comfortable with herself, her guests, and those kids that guests can't help but be sucked into her world and her warmth.

The common thread that weaves these five stories together: George, Shirley, Phillip, Suzanne, and Eloise each have a positive attitude and a cheerful outlook on life. When we first noticed that our highly successful retirees all had similar positive attitudes, we wondered if the trait was learned or if our participants were born under a lucky star. As it turns out, the people we view as lucky—those who seem to sail through life with a smile, no matter the hardships they face—are not that way owing to happenstance. These people have subconsciously or consciously worked on developing a positive attitude toward life.

Research has found that happy people have a particular mind-set. They often have a history and track record of multiple successful past outcomes, but they aren't afraid to take risks or to fail. They have an expectation of continued success, so one setback is not viewed as a tragedy, just a bump in the road to maneuver around. Optimists are willing to experiment with different ways of doing things, and they take calculated risks if they think outcomes will be positive or fruitful. They tend to be gregarious, with an openness that allows them to accept constructive criticism, implement outside suggestions, and change their own behavior if they think it will change an outcome. The happy person gets more "hits" in life because he or she is purposefully positioned to come to bat more often, and is hopeful about striking the ball. Optimism is not associated with intelligence, academic achievement, or wealth. You're in control; you make the choice. *In other words, happiness is a skill you can learn.*

It's a good thing that you can train your brain to be happy because many scientists view a person's emotional state as one of the most important variables when predicting overall long-term good health. Researchers confirm that retirees with a positive attitude and optimism are healthier and live longer. One recent study found that people with positive attitudes lived an average of 7.5 years longer than people who had negative outlooks. This was true regardless of age, gender and socioeconomic status.

Esther Sternberg, M.D., author of *The Balance Within: The Science Connecting Health and Emotion,* says that the immune and nervous systems communicate with each other, creating a clear link between emotions and disease. In response to stressful or "negative" emotions such as anger or fear, the body secretes stress hormones, which make the heart and lungs work faster, tighten muscles, slow digestion, and elevate blood pressure. Pessimists are more likely to frequently excrete stress hormones, and, according to Sternberg, depression and physical illnesses are likely to follow prolonged negativity. On the other hand, positive emotions promote health and faster healing and recovery because positive emotions create immune system antibodies.

As Luck Would Have It

A classic joke goes this way: "LOST DOG: *Right ear missing due to dogfight; left leg missing—caught in bear trap; lost right eye from thorn injury; lost tail in a lawn mower accident; and lost manhood jumping over a barbed-wire fence. Answers to the name of Lucky.*" Like the best humor, this story has more than a grain of truth to it: We all know people like Lucky who seem to have everything going for them, no matter what befalls them.

We admit that retraining your brain to be optimistic isn't easy. Formed by years of personal behavior patterns, our mind-set is deeply interconnected with many parts of our personality, and creates something called our *explanatory style.* University of Pennsylvania professor Martin Seligman, Ph.D., author of *Learned Optimism* and a leader in the field of positive psychology, defines explanatory style as a way of thinking about the cause of situations in our lives or how we explain why things happens to us the way they do. Explanatory styles can run the gamut from highly optimistic, the belief that the future holds promise, to pessimistic, the belief that the future will bring negative outcomes. Seligman argues that our explanatory style is formed during childhood, and unless deliberate steps are taken to change a negative style, it will last a lifetime, affecting the way we relate in the world.

> *In later life, we have essentially two choices. Either we can grow more conservative, more negative, more self-centered, more apprehensive, more narrow-minded, more opinionated, and more argumentative. Or we can reach out and be more helpful, more interested in others, more dedicated to helping and serving others, more tolerant, more forgiving, and more fun to be with. In other words, as I see it we have a choice. I realize that it takes effort but I know that there is a road to greater happiness and a feeling of self-worth and that's where I plan to travel.*
>
> —RETIREMENT DOCS' SURVEY

Here's an everyday extreme example of a pessimist and an optimist but one we can all relate to:

Joan, a pessimist, is in the grocery store and realizes she is in a very long line. She berates herself for being stupid enough to go to the grocery store at a busy time, knowing she will now be late for her next appointment. She feels trapped. Her day is ruined! Why does she always end up in the slowest lines? She directs her anger at the clerk, who seems to be purposely working as slowly as possible and engaging in inane prattle with customers. She's irritated at the people around her, shooting them angry looks. Mostly, though, Joan is mad at herself. In fact, she is so distraught by the time she gets to the clerk that she's close to tears. It takes her fifteen minutes of sitting in the parking lot to cool down and compose herself. She realizes that her two-fisted bangs on the steering wheel did nothing to aid in her angst. Now she's later than even she expected to her next meeting. When she finally arrives, Joan is completely flustered, unhappy, and disorganized.

There's also an optimist, Gail, stuck in the same line, right in back of Joan. She knows that there's probably a shorter line, and she should have looked around for it, but this is where she is, so she'll make the best of it. Gail uses the waiting time to make a to-do list, catch up on a couple of phone calls, and glance through *O,* Oprah's magazine, which is right there in the rack in front of her. By the time she's next in line, she has found a recipe she's been searching for; called her cousin in Cincinnati and a client in New York; and planned her weekend activities. The wait seemed to go by very quickly. Gail might be a few minutes late for her next appointment, but she's also called ahead to let them know she's running behind. They are, too, as it turns out! So everything has worked out perfectly.

While the grocery story scenario is a simplified example of how different explanatory styles can impact our lives, it's also a very real one. In short, how we tend to react to and resolve problems in general can be changed depending on how we look at a set of circumstances—whether it is a traumatic event or just an everyday irritation.

A positive attitude is not something that happens to you; it is a deliberate choice, which ultimately becomes habit. You are positive by deciding in advance that you will always choose the most resourceful response to any given set of circumstances . . . even if you are justified otherwise you will always take the high road . . . in a manner consistent with the goals you want to reach and the person you want to become.

—SUCCESS COACH AND AUTHOR TOM NEWBERRY

THE RESPONSE FACTOR

As geriatric doctors, we are often the bearer of life-changing, life-threatening, and/or fatal pronouncements. When we deliver news of a major illness, we find that after a patient's initial shock and normal short-term depression, the variability of responses is striking, depending on whether the person is a pessimist or an optimist. Optimists see situations as things caused outside of themselves, as temporary and owing to specific reasons. An optimistic patient may respond to bad news something like this: "Hey, I didn't expect to make it this far! I'm thankful to have any years left," or "I'm happy to take whatever time I can get." Pessimists, on the other hand, tend to feel that events are caused either by their behaviors or by outside forces beyond their control, which are working to destroy them. Pessimistic patients tend to give up, give in to depression and/or substance abuse, and respond something like "It figures. What's the point of living?"

Our estimation of recovery and survival rates for each of these two types of patients is very different. The optimist has a better chance of living better and longer than his pessimistic counterpart. Optimists will continue to take care of their health and seek out support from family and friends, whereas the depressed patient might "forget" to take important medicines, begin eating badly, and stop reaching out to family and friends. The extended longevity and better quality of life of the happy patient are precisely why having an optimistic outlook is so crucial as we age: The ability to accept and work through traumatic or stress-causing events, which happen more frequently as we age, and to treat them as temporary and specific, allows optimistic individuals to see their behaviors' positive effect on the outcome of their world. By compartmentalizing each component, we are able to behave in a proactive manner.

When someone generally believes that he or she is helpless and at the mercy of a cruel world, the occurrence of a traumatic event can appear to be daunting and of global proportion. The person reacts, thinking the bad outcome will last forever, and allows himself or herself to be ruled by thoughts of regret, as in "If only I'd done something different." Often completely overwhelmed, the person lacks the ability to actively participate in self-improvement and move through and past the event. If you are overwhelmed with feelings of hopelessness and loss, you tend to neglect physical as well as mental health.

A highly successful university baseball coach said he primarily recruited only high school players who came from strong, winning programs. He felt these kids only knew success, so would work extra hard to avoid failure.

—RETIREMENT DOCS' INTERVIEW

One of our patients, Maria, a stable and attractive seventy-two-year-old woman, is the mother of three successful grown children. Over the past five years we had watched her grow more and more depressed as a result of a series of events. It began with prolonged caregiving responsibilities involving her aged and senile mother. Her own chronic arthritic pain grew more severe with the passing years, and then the unexpected death of her mate took what little wind was left in her sails. Maria felt overwhelmed and helpless by the bad hand life had dealt her over the course of just a few years. With the help of her family and her doctors, she was able to see that life was still worth living—her children loved her and needed her. She had grandchildren who adored her. Maria's arthritis was treatable, and, in fact, with the right course of therapy she regained a lot of movement and dexterity in her hands. An appropriate prescription antidepressant also helped, as did developing a strong support system of friends. It became easier for her to realize how much better off she was than many of her peers and to regain her optimistic attitude.

Some good news for optimists (and for pessimists, too): Exposure to life's unavoidable traumas actually appears to prepare you for the feelings of helplessness that can come from old age. That is, major setbacks occurring anytime during a first career, which you are able to overcome, give you the confidence you need to meet traumatic events in retirement's phases two, three, and four. But if you can't find at least a glimmer of something positive that emerges from the traumatic event, chances are that your negative feelings will grow and you will only become more jaded as you age. That's why cultivating a positive attitude through your whole life is so important. It helps you find the hope and courage to move when you are faced with adversity. In retirement, it's even more important because it's inevitable that there will be more hurdles at this stage of your life. We want you to be able to jump over them!

Another one of our patients, Barbara, explained how her feelings about despair and moving on had changed through a life-altering experience. She had known a couple who had lost their sixteen-year-old son in a car accident. Both parents were understandably devastated, she explained. The father gave up his dental practice and moved to a small cabin in a remote area.

He just couldn't get on with his life. The boy's mother joined her husband for a while but at one point came to acknowledge that her son was gone, and though she would mourn his loss forever, she was still alive. Her husband was unable to come to terms with his grief.

Eventually the woman found it necessary to leave her husband and re-build her life on her own. Barbara said that when her own son was killed in a similar accident, she remembered that couple and their different reactions and made a conscious decision to follow the path that the mother took, as opposed to the father. Yes, she was crushed by the death of her son, but be-cause Barbara was naturally an optimist, she had the strength to continue living a productive life and, in doing so, honored the life of her son. "Lit-tle did that boy's mother know that her decisions, made long before my own, provided me with some insight to move on with my own life," she explained.

YOU HAVE THE POWER TO BE POSITIVE

Why choose to be optimistic? As we've discussed, there are sound scientific facts linking an optimistic outlook to a positive mood, a positive morale, perseverance, effective problem solving, excellent social skills, and good mental and physical health. Simply put, thinking good equals feeling good. Optimistic people take more risks, but that makes sense; they feel confident in their decisions—they believe they will succeed. But, most important, op-timistic people remain open to all of life's possibilities, which is so important to successful aging and retirement. And as you age, this becomes more and more important. Too many of us seem willing to shut down and let our pas-sion and interests slip away later in life. If you have a positive outlook, how-ever, you'll find the courage to open your mind and take on new challenges and adventures—we've known seventy-somethings who've moved to Eu-rope and the Caribbean, learned to ski, and written a play and had it pro-duced. You can do whatever you can dream up—with the right attitude!

DIAGNOSIS

Listed below are some questions to help you discover where you lie on the optimistic-pessimistic spectrum. Think carefully about each of them and how they apply to you. Remember, these are building blocks, and they are all about you and your retirement success.

1. Did your parents value strong character, emotions, and happiness?
   - Yes
   - No
   - Somewhat

2. Do you feel that despite challenges, you will remain hopeful about your future?
   - Yes
   - No
   - Somewhat

3. Do you feel that you are a confident person?
   - Yes
   - No
   - Somewhat

4. Do you believe that your way of doing things will work out for the best?
   - Yes
   - No
   - Somewhat

5. Do you have a clear picture of what you want to happen in your future?
   - Yes
   - No
   - Somewhat

6. Do you know that you will succeed with the goals you set for yourself?
   ◼ Yes
   ◼ No
   ◼ Somewhat

7. If you experience a bad outcome, can you focus on the next opportunity and plan to do better?
   ◼ Yes
   ◼ No
   ◼ Somewhat

8. Did your grade school and high school teachers have lasting positive influences on your adult decision-making?
   ◼ Yes
   ◼ No
   ◼ Somewhat

9. Did your teachers have any negative influence on your adult decision-making?
   ◼ Yes
   ◼ No
   ◼ Somewhat

10. Have you recovered from a major trauma in your life and learned something beneficial during and from it?
    ◼ Yes
    ◼ No
    ◼ Somewhat

11. When negative information comes your way, can you process it thoroughly and apply it to your goal-setting to make it a success?
    ◼ Yes
    ◼ No
    ◼ Somewhat

12. Do you think that you are a creative and flexible person?
    ■ Yes
    ■ No
    ■ Somewhat

If you answered most of the questions with "yes," you have a naturally optimistic explanatory style and will find it easier to maintain it as you age. If you circled mostly "no" and "somewhat" and just a few "yes" answers, you have to work hard to change what could well be a negative attitude. It won't be easy, but with mindfulness and concentration (see our suggestions and exercises later in the chapter), you can improve your disposition by at least 50 percent—this is significant! However, even if you have positive answers for all of the above questions, be aware that in all likelihood, you will experience multiple traumatic situations as you age that can leave you emotionally stretched and overloaded. When bad things happen when we are young, they usually don't happen frequently and we have the wherewithal to recover from them.

As we age, even starting as early as our fifties, traumas occur more frequently, starting with the loss of our job (even if it's voluntary), the loss of friends (whether because they move away or die), and our own increased propensity toward injury and illness, giving us less and less time to recover between events. The impact of those traumas can be reduced if you know that such things are bound to happen as an inevitable part of life and accept them as natural. If you can manage to develop such an attitude toward the rest of your life, we guarantee that you will enjoy it more, no matter what.

THE RETIREMENT DOCS' PRESCRIPTION

If you didn't respond positively to the diagnosis statements, there are simple things you can do to increase your positive attitude. But they take consistent daily practice and patience:

1. **Promise to be positive.** Each morning when you rise, look at yourself in the mirror and commit to being positive just for the day. If necessary, write down "I will be positive" on a piece of paper and tape it to your mirror so you see it everyday. This sounds pretty corny, but you will be surprised at how effective it is in reminding yourself to get the day off to a good start.

2. **Take a moment.** When something happens that you would normally react negatively to (a long line in the grocery store, a rude driver, a depressing phone call from a friend), don't judge it right away as a bad thing. Take a minute and stop yourself from having a bad thought. Changing negative beliefs or opinions into positive ones requires either challenging your pessimistic thoughts and disputing them or distracting yourself from them with a replacement positive thought or activity. Focus on something else or write down any negative thoughts and look back over them later.

3. **Congratulate yourself.** At the end of the day, review what happened and how you reacted. Pat yourself on the back for maintaining a positive outlook and be honest with yourself regarding less-than-positive reactions you may have had. How could you have changed them?

Your goal should be to get to the point where you do not have to actively pause and think about your explanatory style in every situation. But until then, practice the three steps above until reacting positively or at least nonjudgmentally becomes second nature. It may take a while, and you may have to practice the three exercises occasionally. In time, you will develop an ongoing optimistic point of view that will become habit.

We also recommend that you read Martin Seligman's book *Learned Optimism*. He describes the process as a simple look at your ABCs. *A* represents the Adversity we encounter. Perception of the adversity is not established on facts but rather on *B*, our Beliefs, which are based on our upbringing and our past experiences and which are usually habitual. These

beliefs are directly linked to what we feel and eventually to how we will react, causing *C,* the Consequences. We can, with daily practice, learn to
change our beliefs and, as a result, change our reactions and consequences.

Similar to our three simple exercises above, Seligman recommends that
you consciously examine the links among Adversity, Belief, and Consequences and what they mean to the quality of your life. He urges people to
look inward when faced with a positive or negative event and to analyze the
effect they have on it and on their own frame of mind. For instance, when
someone pays you an unexpected compliment, your whole day may improve just because the praise made you feel loved, wanted, and appreciated.
Likewise, a criticism or thoughtless gesture might make you feel angry, depressed, or unworthy for an entire day. If we can recognize that it is not the
external events that make our mood (such as pleasant or unpleasant comments) but our own reaction to them, we can learn to control our responses.

Your own explanatory style is so ingrained in your unconscious that
there's a good chance you may not even notice that you are explaining
events as permanent, pervasive, and personal. As you make a determined
effort to notice your own beliefs and behaviors, you may discover pessimism
of which you may not have been aware. If you can identify the cause of an
adverse situation, recognize your beliefs regarding it, and then examine the
consequences of your beliefs, you are identifying a means to a positive end.
Doing so requires active *engagement,* which in turn results in a positive and
dynamic approach to solving life's events.

THE GRATITUDE ATTITUDE

A positive outlook usually includes a sense of gratitude or thankfulness regardless of life's circumstances. In psychology, gratitude is thought of as an
emotional state, while most religions regard it as a virtue. An attitude of
gratitude may be one way we are able to turn a tragedy into some form of
opportunity for spiritual growth. Think about mourning the loss of a family member, while at the same time experiencing a sense of gratitude for

other family members still alive. Gratitude seems to be an essential element in holding a declining life together. You'll find the need to incorporate it in most religions and self-help organizations. Just look at Alcoholics Anonymous and its success. Like developing a positive outlook, we can increase our awareness of gratitude by practicing some simple techniques, which are taken from cognitive therapy:

1. Identify your nongrateful thoughts. Are they logical? Most of the time they aren't. ("No one loves me." "I've got nothing to do.")

2. Formulate gratitude-supportive thoughts. ("I have some very dear friends and healthy, happy children." "I have free time to pursue what I like.")

3. Substitute grateful thoughts for nongrateful ones.

4. Translate your inner feeling into outward actions. ("I have a few cherished friends" should translate into giving them a call, sending them a note, or making plans to see them. Recognizing that you have free time should result in making a plan to do something that you want to do—start or finish a craft project, read a book, see a movie, etc.)

Our research demonstrated just how important planning and goal orientation are in terms of developing or enhancing a positive attitude. Write to-do lists and stick to them, whether the goals are short- or long-term. Planning, exploration, and spontaneity are not mutually exclusive concepts. Running lists are a way of solidifying things you want to try to accomplish. There are many people who approach their futures with a sense of adventure and a desire to take on new challenges. Try it—it takes a positive attitude to regularly exercise your creativity and stay open to new ideas, new projects, and new stimuli. The payoff—an ever-enriching, involving, and evolving you—lasts right into a healthier, happier ripe old age.

It is always in season for old men to learn.
—AESCHYLUS

The psychologist and University of Chicago professor Mihaly Csikszent-mihalyi wrote about remaining creative as we age in his excellent book *Creativity: Flow and the Psychology of Discovery and Invention.* Part of continuing to be creative, he writes, is in stretching ourselves by continually challenging our problem-solving skills with new questions and in attaining new, more difficult goals, even if they are ultimately unattainable. The more complex the problem, says Csikszentmihalyi, the better.

If you're always doing the "same old, same old," not only will you be bored but your brain muscles will atrophy. Some of the most significant artists and thinkers didn't even get started on exciting new ideas or achieve wide recognition until they were in their second stage of life—their positive attitude helped propel them to try out new ideas. The inventor Buckminster Fuller found fame and almost-cult status among young people in his seventies; the dog trainer Barbara Woodhouse famously said, "Life for me began at seventy," after becoming a TV celebrity; and Colonel Sanders founded his fried chicken empire in his sixties!

Use some of these Csikszentmihalyi-inspired tips to bring new adventures and challenges into your life:

1. **Stay curious.** Don't think you know all the answers. Creative people question the most obvious or seemingly obvious situations. Do not take refuge in the television, radio, newspaper, or pointless conversations. Seek out literature, people, and places that force you to ask questions and form opinions.

2. **Start each day with a specific goal, and end the day trying to come up with a more complex goal for the following day.** Before you retire for the night, think of one thing you want to do the next day. Make it something to look forward to—whether it be seeing a new movie, taking a new car for a test-drive, or researching a trip to a place you have never been before.

3. **Pay attention to what you are doing.** This sounds a lot easier than it actually is. When you engage in any activity, whether it is shopping for groceries, cleaning the house, or driving a car, *be present in the moment.* Focus just on what you are doing—and take in all that is around you. When you do this, you start to see the world differently, notice details that had escaped your attention before, and watch new ideas develop.

4. **Make a fantasy list, and then start checking it off.** Write down ten things you have never done before but would like to try—from the simple (shop at a new store, explore a new walking path) to the silly (ride a Ferris wheel, throw water balloons with your grandson, daughter, niece, or nephew) to the sublime (take a flying lesson, learn to play an instrument). Then, every week, do one of those things so that you can cross it off the list. When you are done with that list, make another one.

Finally, a positive attitude will, of course, help motivate you to develop and maintain all the other important traits for a highly successful retirement. We're not talking about being Pollyanna-happy and cheerful as much as we're talking about an attitude of hopefulness and possibility. It's essential if you want to develop highly successful retirement traits.

It is not the load that breaks you down, it is how you carry it.

—ANONYMOUS

5

TRAIT THREE:
GO WITH THE FLOW—
ACCEPT CHANGE

He who rejects change is the architect of decay. The only human institution which rejects progress is the cemetery.

—HAROLD WILSON, BRITISH POLITICIAN

At the age of twenty, Harriet Doerr interrupted her studies at Stanford University to get married. Forty-five years later, after she had raised two children as a stay-at-home mother, her husband died. Three years after that, her son Michael urged her to go back to college and complete her degree. She did. Doerr was old enough to be her fellow students' grandmother, but the difference in age did not stop her from easily befriending them. In fact, she became one of the gang, often joining her classmates for a beer or a burger after a long day. Her writing professor noticed that Doerr had a remarkable talent and challenged her to write a book, which she did.

Stones for Ibarra was the result, and it was published in 1984, when Doerr was seventy-three. The memoir won the National Book Award and became an international best seller—and Doerr became a literary sensation. Her second book, *Consider This, Señora,* was published in 1993 and also became a best seller. *The Tiger in the Grass,* a collection of stories and anecdotal pieces, was published in 1995, the year her son died of cancer. In her eighties, some devastating changes in her life took place: the loss of her beloved son and severe glaucoma that dramatically impaired her eyesight. Doerr shifted from writing to speaking, and continued to accept invitations to speak about her life and career. She died in 2002 at age ninety-two.

Doerr once remarked, "I operate from chaos," which to us signals a person who not only adapts to change but looks forward to it and embraces it. No wonder she was able to accomplish so much in the last twenty-five years of her life—more than most people accomplish in a lifetime. And this was after already living one life and raising a family!

We all know at least one survivor similar to Doerr, a person who responds to setbacks and change (the death of a spouse or a child) by adapting to the circumstances (going back to school as a senior citizen, mastering a skill like writing, speaking to others about her life experiences) and succeeding. Even those who live through a plethora of adversity—consider Abraham Lincoln, whose life was beset by tragedy and failure but who became one of our most revered presidents—seem to have been born with built-in endurance machines. But that's not the case. Social scientists label the capacity to cope with hindrances and challenges and to rise above them *resilience*.

Long-lived people as a group are strongly resilient; that characteristic is one of the reasons they make it to their eighties and nineties, or beyond. Resilient people can handle trauma and accept change. Our Retirement Docs' Survey data reaffirmed that accepting change becomes a priority particularly in retirement in phase two, when coping with the loss of full-time work and the professional and social satisfaction we derived from it can be and often is devastating, and in phases three and four, when the loss of loved ones and other major setbacks occur more frequently.

Fortunately, we can build up our resiliency and teach ourselves to deal with repeat upsets even if they happen in quick succession or simultaneously—for example, the loss of a job, workplace friends, regular income, and/or sense of purpose. Overall, self-confidence, decision-making ability, and a sense of independence are part of a resilient person's makeup. While many of these qualities are developed during childhood in secure and loving families led by caring and thoughtful parents, even people who had tough upbringings can learn to be resilient. If you think you are one of those people, and you're reading this book, our bet is that you are resilient and can become even more so.

PHASES TWO AND THREE— SURVIVING THE TRANSITION FROM JOB TO JOBLESS

Retiring from a job can be as heart-wrenching and shocking as being fired. One day you get up at 6:00 A.M. to get the 7:05 into the office, and the next you're up early wondering what to do with the next twelve hours. If you are not resilient, this is a scenario ripe for negative behavior and plummeting self-esteem. If you visualize yourself having a tough time going from working to wandering, you can make some preemptive strikes to soften the blow. As we discussed in chapter three, talk to your employer; see if it's possible to ease out of your workplace slowly—see if you can create a smooth transition for yourself from your company. There's a chance that with your expertise you can cut back on hours but stay on, doing something like keeping track of a project for a month or two—or as an on-call consultant or mentor. Make a list of ways you see yourself remaining valuable to your employer, whether you work for a huge company, in a small establishment, or for yourself.

RESILIENT PEOPLE HAVE CONTINGENCY PLANS

There will be a chance that your company doesn't have a place for you, and there may be a moment in between work and settling into a new routine or another job or business when you will find yourself facing a vacuum of time and autonomy. There is a solution for getting through this period. The advantageous difference between getting fired or laid off and retiring is that you know you are going to retire, and you usually know when. While some of us are thrilled to retire, others are not. If you are one of the latter, you can prepare and be ready to deal with and head off possible feelings of anger, shame, resentment, bitterness, and grief that can be a result of leaving a job or that may occur after the "honeymoon" period (those first few weeks or months after retirement), when you stop enjoying the sense of freedom you first felt when calling it quits. First of all, recognize that it is not unusual to experience resentment and hurt when you retire. We're not saying that you will have these feelings, but if you do, you are not alone. Many other fellow retirees feel the same way. Put a resiliency-building plan to work before you retire.

1. **Give yourself time to grieve.** You worked your whole life! Chances are good that you're going to feel bad about giving up a job and daily contact with individuals who mean a lot to you. Recognize that grieving is not the same as wallowing or feeling like a victim. Resilient people grieve for their loss; they don't blame their circumstance.

2. **Write and talk about it.** James Pennebaker, a psychologist at Southern Methodist University in Dallas and author of *Writing to Heal: A Guided Journal for Recovering from Trauma and Emotional Upheaval*, has found in numerous studies that people who confide their feelings, either to themselves in the form of a journal, or to a close friend or confidant, are better able to bounce back from trauma and have healthier immune systems.

3. **Create a new community.** You may be able to stay in touch with your former friends from work, but it won't be easy and it won't be the same, especially if you socialized with them only during your working hours. As the saying goes, "life goes on," and that's what's happening. The life they know marches forth and yours is no longer a part of that makeup. Attempting to hang on doesn't build resiliency. Have you seen the movie *About Schmidt,* in which Jack Nicholson plays the role of a new retiree? Disengage from your old job by seeking out a new bunch of "colleagues" to hang out with. One way of doing this is via social service and community volunteering. If you can't

or don't want to find a paying job, use your work skills to help society and create a new professional situation for yourself. Re-create the intrinsic qualities that made your first career meaningful.

4. **Ease out over time.** Do your skills translate into other jobs that can help you ease away from working altogether? One government researcher we know became a high school math teacher at a charter school for science and math in New Jersey after retiring from her Washington, D.C., job. Eventually, she retired from that, too, and lived happily ever after tutoring children in math after school, until she couldn't wait to not have to work at anything anymore. Now she travels, reads books, and simply enjoys the sunsets. She got over the need to work; she just took about fifteen years doing so.

PHASE FOUR—FACING THE CHALLENGES OF OLD AGE

It's a given, if we live long enough, that we will all face a series of major life-altering adversities, often with little or no recovery time in between. Advanced age brings with it a lot of baggage that needs to be recognized and managed. It's possible as elders that we could lose a spouse, deal with a sick loved one, become sick ourselves, and find it necessary to offer emotional support to a grown child who might have a crisis of his or her own, and all of this at the same time. Numerous changes can potentially overwhelm our basic resilience. Other major roadblocks that occur in phase four include our loss of independence, decreased stamina, decreased mobility, and the potential inability to care for ourselves by ourselves. Add to the lineup the developing major body changes linked directly to aging, chronic diseases, and decreased memory, hearing, and eyesight. Not our favorite list by far, but for each probable condition (every one of them a traumatic event), it's so important to be alert and ready with robust and ready resilience. Resilience rules! Resilience to the rescue! Tape that to your mirror too!

DIAGNOSIS

Here are some questions to ask yourself relating to the strength of your own resiliency factor, also known as the ability to accept change:

■ Did a caring family raise you?
■ Did your childhood incorporate religious, ethnic, and/or cultural beliefs?
■ Overall, do you feel you've made positive decisions in your lifetime and have good problem-solving skills?
■ Do you have a strong sense of spirituality?
■ Do you have strong feelings of self-worth and confidence?
■ Have you faced major traumas in your lifetime and generally recovered well?
■ Are you able to accept change, even at the last minute?
■ Are you merciful, as opposed to trying to get even?

This is just a glimpse at the complex characteristics of resiliency. If you answered yes to these questions, you are most likely a naturally resilient person. If you responded with negatives, you need to work hard at developing a resilient nature. If you want to do further resiliency-related research, an excellent book is *The Resilience Factor,* by Karen Reivich, Ph.D., and Andrew Shatte, Ph.D. In the meantime, our prescription for resilience, if practiced daily, should help you learn to bounce back and better. Take as needed.

THE RETIREMENT DOCS' PRESCRIPTION

Retirement and aging are inevitable. Understand that certain traumas are a part of the normal cycle of life. It is never too late to teach yourself to be a highly successful change survivor. Acknowledging that your life will change, coupled with a realistic attitude, leads to acceptance and ease of stress, which in turn add to basic resilience patterns. If you can develop a Harriet Doerr–like mind-set and embrace change and thrive on chaos, instead of running away from it or denying it, you can give yourself a "heads-up" advantage for coping.

Practice the following skills to shore up your resilience reserves. This is *not* a short-term process. You've got to keep at it. The ability to accept change is an ongoing, lifelong, ever-evolving skill.

1. **Develop and maintain an independent spirit.** Even if you have friends and family nearby, you still need a sense of self-determination and self-sufficiency. Resilient people can take care of themselves. They can do things on their own and enjoy it. Practice by solving a problem by yourself, taking in a movie or dining in a restaurant solo, or taking a trip on your own—and enjoying it. There will be many times when you will be alone after you retire—if you don't enjoy your own company, you're in trouble. Think again about Harriet Doerr and people like her whom you know—off she went to college at sixty-five, all by herself! Take responsibility for your actions. If physical disabilities linked to age create a loss of external controls, let them go. Transfer your energy into maintaining your internal reins. Resist letting other people do tasks for you if with a little extra effort you can accomplish them by yourself. Be in charge of your day-to-day life, and don't waste time on things that you can't control. And don't forget, blame only prolongs personal recovery processes.

2. **Cultivate insight.** This is the mental habit of asking yourself tough questions and answering them honestly. It entails moving away from being self-centered and toward being outwardly directed, trying to see the things from someone else's point of view. This can prevent you from falling into the "why me" and "everybody is against me" trap. Viewing the world as cruel or unjust may be simply growing old and feeling a frightening lessening of control, which in turn can create depression. No one we've ever met has liked feeling out of control, but again, it's a given. As you age, you're going to feel you're losing some

of your power. Becoming a senior citizen is not someone else's fault. It's real life marching you through your very own timetable.

3. **Get help.** Yes, we did just tell you to become independent. Yet independent people know when to ask for outside help—this is not the same thing as leaning on friends or family members for obligatory companionship or enforced "amuse-me" sessions. Resilient people participate in relationships, understand that they are a two-way street, and are willing to actively participate in the give-and-take necessary to make a relationship gratifying, not only for them but also for other people. Resilience researchers also say that strong, flexible people are not afraid to talk about obstacles or challenges with a professional, a confidant, a clergyperson, or a friend.

If I don't see one of my children every day, one or two of us will get in touch by phone. And now I'm e-mailing my grandchildren with thoughts on my long life. It makes me feel that I'm contributing emotional support, valuable memories of life's experiences, as well as keeping up with day-to-day involvements. I feel a real ongoing connection. I'm old, but I'm not unhappy. My family has become my life. They make me feel that they need me, and I know I sure need them.

—RETIREMENT DOCS' SURVEY

4. **Reframe your life and experiences.** Take a look at your life now and your history, and put them in perspective. You've survived this long—there has got to be a reason for it! If you can see why and how you "made it" this far, you can see your own strengths and achievements clearly. Basically, this is consciously taking a glass-half-full approach to life, as opposed to a glass-half-empty one. Make a list of your accomplishments—from bringing up happy children to making a contribution at your job to being a helpful neighbor—and see these things for what they are: the sum total of a brave and well-lived life. Make a list of "retirement advantages" so that you can visualize all the great things about not having to work anymore—everything from sleeping late during the week to traveling wherever and whenever

you like. An "advantages list" is a deceptively simple yet powerful way to reframe your situation.

5. **Create your life plan and refer to it often.** Getting a clear idea of who you are, how you want your life to operate, and how you see yourself in the future provides a fall-back strategy when you're faced with trauma or unexpected events. For example, plot out your responses to an illness in your family or to your own illness. Devise a scheme for when you want to move from where you are living. Be as concrete as possible, but also know that such plans can be revised. Respect yourself; capitalize on your own personal assets, your own uniqueness. Review your life plan on an ongoing basis, particularly following a stressful event. Does it provide the resilience and the psychological well-being you need to get back on track, or is it time to adjust and update? Comparing yourself to other people who have experienced adversities similar to yours will give you a sense of yourself, where you are now, and where you want to be. And remember, because this is your life plan, it's all about you—make it work for you.

I have noticed that some retired business leaders do not do well when faced with irreversible adversity. As captains of industry, they were able to correctly identify a problem. If they didn't know the answer, they consulted with others who would.

Now in retirement, their problems have no clear solutions, and these former leaders have more difficulty adjusting. They have lost control, as well as the knowledge of how to react.

—RETIREMENT DOCS' INTERVIEW

6. **Simplify.** In general, the older you get, the fewer balls you can keep in the air without dropping one or two of them. Why struggle to juggle? Unnecessary but stressful tasks, annoying chores, and irritating people, places, and things can erode your resiliency. This is the time to enjoy and spend time doing things you like. Retirement is all about eliminating tasks that you never enjoyed in the first place. What can you do to rid yourself of them? One consideration is maintaining "the

family home"—when most of the family has long vacated. The fact that your children (now most of them with their own kids) love making those memory-lane visits to "their house" or their life as it was is a great compliment to you, and we're not saying that you don't enjoy all the memories attached too. But what *was* isn't, and a good-sized home can easily become a drag as well as a big drain on you. Sell it! Free yourself from stress: moving to a location that requires less upkeep and provides a secure environment makes a lot of sense. Another stress reducer: eliminate annoying reading material, as well as radio and television programs if you know they will upset rather than inspire you. A liberal probably doesn't want to start the day listening to Rush Limbaugh. On the other hand, if controversy and politics excite you, that's not stress, that's positive energy! Make a conscious effort to distinguish which media are pleasurable for you to engage in and those that make you angry or unhappy so you know what to avoid. Likewise, if your cousin Millie's husband David makes you nuts, don't feel forced to spend time with him. Associate with the people you like and who make you feel great. The point is to be mindful about who and what makes you happy and put your energies and focus there.

From the beginning of time, the ability to adjust to change has been the basis for survival for all living things.

—RETIREMENT DOCS

6

Trait Four: A Little Help from Your Friends (and Family)—the Strong Support Group

Let us be grateful to people who make us happy; they are the charming gardeners who make our souls blossom.

—Marcel Proust

Human beings are not meant to live solitary lives. We are social creatures by nature, and maintaining close ties with family and friends becomes even more vital to our well-being after we retire. Our highly successful retirees overwhelmingly stated that close social and family relationships made their lives richer, happier, and more meaningful. But they also said they had to work at maintaining them. In the first half of our lives, up until our late forties and early fifties, family and social relationships are easy to maintain. They are truly a balance of give-and-take. Most of us live with or close to our immediate family, and our friends are easy to access at work and in the neighborhood. It's easy to blend personal and professional events and friendships. It's give-and-take in equal measure.

When we retire, there is a greater potential to fall into a social vacuum unless we strive to put ourselves in situations where we interact with family, old friends, and new faces. It requires extra effort on our part. It becomes more of a "give, give, give, and take" than a give-and-take scenario—to stay in touch with our kids, relatives, former friends/coworkers, and friends, who may move away or are just not as easy to reach as in the past, for any number of reasons (perhaps they still work and you don't). You need to watch and work on your social connections as carefully as you supervise your fiscal and health plans.

After my father died, I watched my mother become lonely and depressed. She was without any friends, and had an address book with most of the names crossed out. This made me supersensitive to gathering a wide and varied group of friends and to be emotionally close to my family. In my retirement, I track this much as I do my finances and my health.

—RETIREMENT DOCS' INTERVIEW

Along with a group of our lifelong friends, we all moved to a desert community and bought condos. It was a dream coming true; we had talked for years about retiring together and how perfect it would be. But before long, we found that no matter how close our friendships, some of us moved on to other areas, some developed other interests, some got sick, and, sadly, one in our tight-knit group has died.

My husband and I decided to expand and extend our social circle because we saw that unexpected and unplanned changes could leave us a future without close friends. We've met and formed new friendships with people in our community, and they have become important to us. We now feel that we can never have too many friends, especially at this time in our lives.

—RETIREMENT DOCS' INTERVIEW

Having friends is particularly good for your mental health: it's been known for some time that single and socially isolated people stand a greater chance of developing dementia, including Alzheimer's disease. A study conducted by Robert Wilson at Rush University Medical Center was the first to show a link between people who were lonely or disconnected and a higher risk of developing dementia later in life.

Friends also extend life: Australian researchers conducted a ten-year study of more than fifteen hundred people seventy and older, which concluded in 2002. They found that those who had regular contact, in person or on the phone, with at least five friends, had 22 percent fewer deaths in the following decade than those who had few friends and limited contact with them. According to the researchers, the friends of study participants provided them with a sense of intimacy, shared interests, and support during difficult times.

But as in real life, reality can bite—and the same was not always true of the Australian participants' family members, who often contributed to their stress. We also found this to be true in our research. As one of our respondents wrote:

> *Your support groups no longer have to be in your backyard, not with the caliber of support that you get from e-mails and the telephone. In fact, being geographically close to your kids may be a detriment when you retire. They interfere too much. They try to control your life, and then they try to make you feel guilty if you don't do things they want you to do. And heaven help you if you marry somebody that they don't like. They also interfere during holidays. Living a little ways away is not all bad.*

> —RETIREMENT DOCS' INTERVIEW

Despite the variety of emotions that family relationships often evoke, our mate, siblings, children, and other close relations remain the backbone of our support groups—most of us still rely on family for the give-and-take of emotional, physical, and financial support. Of course, perfect families, no matter what our generation, have always been the exception rather than the rule. But in what other setting can you make mistakes time after time and still be welcome? Where else can you talk openly with one another, even admit, "This family is dysfunctional!" and disagree, shout, laugh, cry, and (most of the time) hug and make up? Having a good family structure comes in shades of success, but a unified family increases all of your chances for happiness in your retirement years. If poor family relationships exist before retirement, they will usually continue after retirement. If this is the case in your family, and if you're getting our message, swallow your pride and at least make an effort to repair things.

Research has shown that a strong support group offers many benefits, including:

- Longer life
- Better mental and physical health
- A stronger immune system
- Quicker recovery from illness and surgery
- The need for fewer medications
- Lower blood pressure
- Fewer visits to doctors
- Feeling loved and highly regarded
- A connection to the community and the world
- Less smoking and alcohol intake
- Easier weight loss

CIRCLE AROUND TO YOUR CIRCLE OF SUPPORT

We like the idea of looking at your relationships as circles emanating around and out from us in an ever-changing and ongoing dynamic process: The people in our lives move from one ring and then back over time. The graphic here shows the entire circle of support, and each one of the four radiating rings is essential in supporting you. Some people will move back and forth among the four rings. But how you manage those circles and your relationship to and with them is central to your well-being.

CIRCLE OF SUPPORT

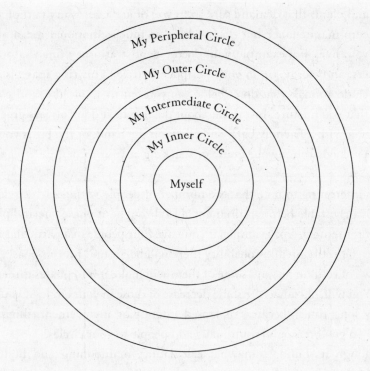

Inner Circle: Your first circle of support includes your intimate relationships, the people you feel so close to that your life without them is
unimaginable. They often include your mate, your children and their
mates, your grandchildren, your great-grandchildren, exceptionally
close friends, and, sometimes, pets.

Intermediate Circle: This second circle of support includes dear friends,
close relatives, and caregivers. After you retire, you have to make more
of an effort to reach out to these people—and try to add new ones.

Outer Circle: The third circle of support fluctuates the most, starting
when you enter phase two of retirement. It's made up of your basic
support groups, people you enjoy being with but don't often see
socially or on a regular basis. It may include acquaintances from religious, social, volunteer, political, and community organizations, as
well as new people you meet and become friendly with.

Peripheral Circle: This outermost circle is made up of people, animals, and plants that demand care from you or are a necessary part of your core maintenance but do not have as much emotional meaning to your lives. For example, your doctor, dentist, attorney, financial advisers, and clergy are in your peripheral circle. This ring may also include animals that don't belong to you but that you like, and plants that you nurture. Just think about the dog next door, always greeting you with a friendly bark and a lick on the hand, or the birds you see perched around your house or snacking at your feeder.

It's interesting to note that the number of people within each circle remains fairly stable before retirement, and throughout phase one and phase two of retirement. For example, if you have four people in a particular ring before you retire, in all probability there will be around four in phases one and two of retirement, and some of them will make it into phases three and four. You will, of course, see some decrease of those in your circles if you live a very long time—because of lapsed interest or involvement, illness or death—a good reason to continually add people to your circles.

Though it sounds somewhat calculating, maintaining and building friendships is really about planning ahead. When you have friends, along with acquaintances you can visualize as replacement friends waiting in the wings, you are building in future helpers for a time when you will really need them—phase three and especially phase four. Developing friendships is even important in phase two, since your spouse may not share every interest you have. Unless we die before our time, mentally and physically, old age asks for more than it's able to give. When our well-being demands active assistance, if we can have it delivered via a ready, willing, helpful, and caring support group, we're going to be a lot better off and a lot happier. Stop and think for a moment. Visualize yourself as old, really old. Shut your eyes and do it. Now, imagine yourself needing hands-on physical assistance with transportation as well as help with social interaction at a nephew's wedding; or day-to-day activities, like a trip to the bathroom; or your finances. How is the scenario looking?

Luckily, field-testing new support systems—also called exploring new friendships and associations—can be fun and will contribute to your zest for life. As you will see in the prescription section of this chapter, there are more options than ever available to meet people who share your interests, and an ever-growing number of clubs and organizations catering to the needs of adults.

After my wife and I married, my focus was limited to family involvement and my profession. I had little time to develop much more than my inner and intermediate circles of support. Over a five- to ten-year period before I entered phase two's semi-retirement with income, I ventured in and out of various potential support groups attempting to develop my outer circles. This was by design. I was preparing myself for decreased time on the job, and I was field-testing possible leisure-time pursuits. Then I fully entered phase two and worked on developing all four of my circles. The backbone of my inner circle remained my mate, our children and their mates, and our grandchildren. Making good friends outside the medical profession has been great fun, but the three major blessings I most enjoy are involvement with our children and our grandchildren, and spending more quality time with my wife.

—Dr. Fritz

I can't recall ever "planning" for a support group. They simply evolved as experiences with family, schooling, hobbies, and career development helped them naturally form. For example, early in my grade school education, a woodworking class attracted me. Learning as much as possible about woodworking led me to explore different disciplines, where I met more and more people as a result of our mutual interest. When I was ten, I started playing golf with neighborhood friends simply because there was a public golf course in our neighborhood. My interest continued through high school and college, and into my adult life. My family and I have been lucky enough to play on courses that in my childhood I only dreamed of. Golf has provided me with ongoing social support made up of both old and new friends. In fact, just last week I was in a foursome made up of those same pals from my childhood—we've never lost touch.

Medical school obviously produced new support groups with professors and colleagues, followed by patient-doctor relationships formed during the years of my practice. I have particularly valued what I learned from my patients.

*My advice for finding your own support groups is to pay attention to what you
love and share in it.*

—DR. JIM

THE INNER CIRCLE: THE FAMILY UNIT
AND ITS MANY FORMS

In common-sense terms, as you get older, your practical needs, both physical and emotional, markedly benefit from a loving and supportive family. A
tolerant and somewhat supportive family is better than none at all. Even
though cultural and economic factors have changed our idea of the traditional American family—currently only 24 percent of us who cohabitate are
married, as compared to 1960, when 52 percent of us living together had
tied the knot—most of us over sixty-five still rely primarily on the traditional family unit for support, as do Baby Boomers. The difference is that
Boomers have added and expanded the definition of family to include a
broader base of people, which can create a less-stable family unit.

Looking over the statistics in the previous paragraph, we realize it's no
wonder that many people born between 1946 and 1964 are having a problem identifying their traditional roots.

MARRIAGE—AND HOW MEN
AND WOMEN RETIRE

For better or for worse, retired couples spend more time with each other and
about 40 percent less time with their friends than they do before they retire.

Like this famous historian, we all hope that we can feel as smitten by a
special someone in our own later decades:

*The love we have in our youth is superficial compared to the love that an old man
has for his wife.*

—WILL DURANT

But, often, couples find that they have different interests once they retire. In the beginning, negotiating these differences can be a trying time in
some marriages. For example, you may be thrilled that you finally have the
time to travel, but your spouse may want to spend his or her carefree days
reading the books he or she never had time to enjoy.

In addition, research shows that men and women have different styles
when it comes to cultivating outside relationships. Women tend to have an
easier experience keeping a social network active when they retire than
men typically do. They, like men, usually have at least one confidant but,
unlike them, often a tight-knit group of best friends. They are by far much
better than men at ongoing social networking, particularly under stressful
conditions. More women go to support groups (whether medically or emotionally based). Women tend to group and men to scatter. As one of our survey respondents explained:

> Some of my girlfriends feel closer to their girlfriends than they do to their hus-
> bands. Their husbands aren't interested in talking to them and, more important,
> listening to them. Their girlfriends are. I think that when a wife loses a husband,
> she may miss him with all her heart but still it seems that she fills her lonely times
> more easily than a man, usually with close friends. From what I've observed,
> more often than not, women have close friends and men have acquaintances.
>
> —RETIREMENT DOCS' SURVEY

Many men often put their careers ahead of maintaining or making new
friends, and as a consequence they lose the skills required to establish or
keep ongoing friendships other than those that are work-related. It's no surprise that following retirement, about a third of men entering phases two
and three spend significantly more time with their families. Fortunately,
many men genuinely look forward to the amounts of time they find available to involve themselves with their mates, children, and grandchildren.
However, if they're doing so out of a new sense of excess time, many of
those new retirees indeed feel lost and, temporarily, directionless.

Most men and their wives adjust to their new roles in time. A six- to
eighteen-month adjustment period is the length of time you can expect

to spend fine-tuning your "new" relationship. Occasionally you may feel as if you're growing apart, not closer, but if you survived a long-term union before retirement, research shows that there is little negative impact on matrimony owing to retirement, at least for most of us. David Ekerdt, a University of Kansas sociologist who studies retirement and aging, and Veterans Administration research sociologist Barbara Vinick found in a study of two hundred couples that retirement did not put relationships into a crisis mode, as was commonly thought. While some women complained that their husbands cramped their style to a certain extent, such as monitoring their daily routines or listening to their telephone conversations, husbands who were home took care of and shared in more jobs around the house, which made their wives very happy. And, after some discussion, most couples eased into the change in everyday routines comfortably.

A good marriage before retirement is generally a good marriage after. It may sound trite, but take time to remember those first "crazy in love" years of your marriage and get back to them. Time, talk, and a couple of tantrums will get you where you need to be to get on with the rest of your life.

One issue to be aware of—research shows that there is the possibility of a significant crossover effect of depression, health problems, and negative events from one partner to the other. This is especially true for the woman, since odds are that she is the more maternal of the two and, statistics show, probably in better health than her mate. It's important to find a balance. Concentrate on providing support and understanding to your spouse while taking care of your own physical and mental health.

Between the ages of sixty-five and seventy-four, 80 percent of men and 55 percent of women are married; after eighty-five, 50 percent of men and only 13 percent of women are married. Up to 60 percent of people over age sixty-five are living alone. With those kinds of statistics, it's important to recognize that either you or your spouse will probably die before the other one does—going out at the same time is not the norm. Make sure you both understand what you want to do and who you want to turn to, including your professional contacts—attorneys, accountants, money managers, insurance agents—and know the roles that they will perform for the surviving partner. This will help take some stress out of your life now as you ponder what the future holds.

TIME WITH GRANDCHILDREN

Of all the activities that couples enjoy doing together, our highly successful retirees ranked visiting grandchildren as number one. Both our own data and data from other studies found no correlation between the actual numbers of children or grandchildren and grandparent happiness. So if you have just one grandchild to lavish all of your attention on, or if you're one of the people jumping up calling out "Twenty-five! Twenty-five! Twenty-five!" when the "How Many Do You Have Now?" contest begins—hurrah for you both. You are equally happy with the most important part of all—they are yours! As grandparents, we can have a lot of influence, but, most important, we've got a lot of bonus playtime waiting to be had. *If you do not have a grandchild, get a pet, or develop a relationship with a niece, nephew, or a friend's child. Having friends of all ages is entertaining and educational.*

How could I not be crazy about my grandchild? My daughter recently sent me this e-mail she received from my three-year-old grandson's Baptist preschool teacher—"God loves me, Jesus loves me, and Grandma loves me." First, he got the order of importance right, and second, he's only three years old and he's already been published!

—RETIREMENT DOCS' SURVEY

For each grandchild's tenth birthday, my late wife and I made a practice of taking him or her individually almost anywhere he or she wanted to go for a three- to ten-day trip. Let me add that we have seen some amazing choices made: Cleveland? Not that we didn't fully enjoy our trip, but at the time it gave us pause. Cleveland versus the pyramids? One of our grandsons was a Cleveland Indians fan and a trip to their ballpark was a dream come true for him and, as it turned out, for us as well. His choice was one of the best of all our vacations, and I might add, Cleveland is a beautiful place to spend some time seeing. This individual bonding experience along with an annual all-family vacation has paid untold dividends for me throughout my life. I'm eighty-six years old, and some of my grandkids are old enough to have grandkids. The nice thing is, they still come and see me. I am in the more lonely late years of my life, and a visit from them sure makes my day.

—RETIREMENT DOCS' SURVEY

CLOSE FRIENDS

In demographic surveys of people born before 1946, respondants rank their mate as the most important source of support in their inner circle, followed by their children, grandchildren, and parents. Only a few included a very close friend. Enter the Baby Boomers, all 77 million of them, and though remaining traditionally reliant on spouses and children for their inner circle support, they more often include a close friend, and sometimes more than one, in their inner circle. Family relationships are, in part, bound by obligation and are virtually permanent. Friendships, on the other hand, are based on mutual consent. They can begin by chance, and they can end whenever the relationship is no longer rewarding.

Recent data suggest that we will live longer if we have very close friends and we are not dependent solely on our families for emotional support, particularly when we're old. It is ideal to have one or two very close friends and many acquaintances. Bleak as it sounds, as those close friends pass away, move, or have emotional or physical disorders associated with age, you need to have a reserve of other people you can depend upon. Just like the loss of a mate, it's not that we ever want to lose what we so much enjoy today, it's just a plain fact of life—it will happen. When you retire, the loss of your mate can be softened if you have an extremely close friend or friends. Digest this information, take a careful look, and do some thinking and planning for your future.

Since the majority of us over the age of sixty do not have a mate, the importance of developing close friendships becomes even more apparent. Take a cue from the single, the divorced, and the widowed; they know that gathering together plays a big part in their family-by-choice life support.

As we grow into retirement's phases three and four, we may relate more easily and more intimately to people who are of similar age and/or with similar infirmities. It's more difficult to talk to a family member about "plumbing problems" and all those other age-related diseases. A close friend or a group of similarly aged elders can understand and offer moral and emotional help—and sometimes even come up with a physical fix that actually works. After all, most of us have "been there, done that" after putting in many years.

INTERMEDIATE AND OUTER-CIRCLE SUPPORT

In the intermediate circle are individuals who are friends, a few of whom may have the potential to come into the inner circle. The outer circle is primarily organizations and/or acquaintances. These two circles also include more-distant friends and relatives.

Society is changing, and more and more leisure activities are becoming solitary: for example, watching television, working on the computer, playing computer games, and plugging in our iPods. No longer are we joiners; all national fraternal organizations and most religions have had a decrease in attendance. Adult athletic programs and bowling leagues are shrinking, and community involvement and almost all areas where you meet, greet, and develop new relationships are diminishing. Consequently, when the Boomers fully retire, many could find themselves with a feeling of not belonging anywhere or having no place to go.

I don't really miss work, but I do miss the people I worked with, the social interchange and feeling of community.

—RETIREMENT DOCS' SURVEY

As a retiree, it's very important to maintain these kinds of social connections. Specific suggestions appear later in this chapter.

PERIPHERAL CIRCLE

This circle includes anybody and anything that requires personal responsibility—for you or from you. This includes your support group of advisers, which your mate should be as familiar with as you are. It will allow a surviving spouse to keep the ongoing business of living intact. This circle also includes living things, such as animals other than your own pets and plants that depend upon your care and feeding. The responsibility and obligation that are parts of these peripheral relationships are actually crucial in keeping you alive and dynamic. They can become part of our "reason to live."

Maintaining a small garden you care about, seeing neighbors and enjoying casual chitchat with them, visiting your attorney or tax accountant or the woman at the bank with whom you discuss your personal business affairs are important simply in terms of continuing the varied nature of everyday life. Daily activities that include others are similar to keeping up with current events or taking in cultural activities. They simply add meaning and depth to life—and in a hands-on sense, going to the dentist, seeing your doctor for a checkup, and checking in with your investment adviser maintain your practical well-being. Losing interest in them is one of the first signs of depression!

> *Every few years my wife and I get together socially with our attorney, accountant, money manager, insurance agent, and pastor. We do it to stay involved with them in a friendly, not an all-business, relationship. We feel that if something were to happen to one of us, the other would feel comfortable and knowledgeable carrying on.*
>
> —RETIREMENT DOCS' SURVEY

THE DIAGNOSIS: HOW STRONG IS YOUR SUPPORT GROUP?

Read through the following list carefully and take time to answer each question. The more affirmative answers you give, the better off you are in terms of your circles of support. However, keep in mind that even if you have an active social life now, you have to continually maintain and add to it.

- Is my mate the most important person in my life?
- Do I have a close relationship with my children?
- Am I in contact with my grandchildren on a regular basis?
- Do I enjoy spending time with my children's mates?
- Do I enjoy helping other people?
- Do I attend church on a regular basis?
- Do I belong to a volunteer group or groups?
- Are there fish, birds, or other pets or animals that I care for?
- Do I have plants or other things that I care for and cultivate?
- Do I enjoy making new friends?
- Do I have at least one very close friend?
- Do I have friends or acquaintances who are both much younger and older than I am?

THE RETIREMENT DOCS' PRESCRIPTION: DEVELOPING AND MAINTAINING SUPPORT GROUPS

Relationships, like plants and pets, will wither and die if not looked after on a regular ongoing basis. Get your inner circle on a "care and feeding schedule" with the following simple tips. Look at your support groups as your own protective shield or your emotional safety-deposit box. Hopefully, you will never have to make demands on it, but if you live long enough, you more than likely will. Your groups are there for your emotional, physical, spiritual, and financial support. Just don't forget—your circles are ever-changing. Their maintenance requires time, effort, understanding, and that most noble of all virtues, forgiveness.

IT'S ALL ABOUT FAMILY

Not only will you be able to create a closer family support network by following the suggestions below, but you will also create a better you. Both are part of achieving a highly successful retirement.

- **Learn to forgive and forget!** Do you even remember how the feud between you and another family member began? Do you have strained relationships with your children or siblings that you need to address? *Now* is the time to act. Your mental health (and theirs) will benefit greatly. Keep in mind that grandchildren and nieces and nephews that you have a special affinity and love for can, by the nature of your relationship with them, become significantly unifying, often making it easier to bring quarreling family members to the same table.
- **Don't be judgmental.** If you are, stop. You'll be amazed at what a good time you can have with your family if you treat them with respect. Work to accept each of them as they are. There's a good chance that they will work just as hard when they see you making an effort to overlook their habits, quirks, and political opinions! You may find yourself receiving a lot of satisfaction by reaching out to a wayward child, grandchild, or other relative.
- **Expand your family circle.** Members outside one's immediate family are often untapped support resources. Aunts, uncles, cousins, in-laws, nieces, and nephews—these are all important relationships to nurture.
- **Be your family's guardian.** Offer your help to them in times of need, whether emotional, economic, or caregiving. If you're there for your

family before retirement, chances are they will be there for you when advanced age-related setbacks come calling.

■ **Gather the family together regularly to celebrate.** Salute birthdays, graduations, promotions, travel plans, and major holidays together. Get everyone involved in planning them—from who will bring the wine to who will make the pasta salad to who will bring the party hats.

■ **Take time away for family vacations.** Enjoy one another away from home. Often, being in a new, restful location eases tensions and helps everyone relax and enjoy one another's company.

MAINTAIN CLOSE FRIENDSHIPS

Friends provide support and understanding in nonjudgmental and unemotional ways that spouses or other family members often cannot—maybe you have a friend who shares your passion for the opera or reads history books with the same voraciousness. Or maybe they are just people you enjoy spending time with, sharing ideas and perspectives, and, most important, sharing a good laugh.

■ **Develop a small number of extremely close friends.** Too many close friends can actually take time away from maintaining closeness. Even one confidant is a major plus, and better than ten friendly acquaintances. It's hard to say exactly how to form close friendships because, like love relationships, close friendships often start with chemistry and go from there. Of course, to have a good friend, one must be a good friend. Once you stop working, the most likely way of finding people who have the potential to become good friends is to put yourself in situations where you will meet others who share your interests, values, and lifestyle. For example, if you like chess, join a chess club. If you love Italy, take an adult education course in Roman history. If you like kayaking, go kayaking with a group.

■ **If you are male and single, make friendships a big priority.** In our experience, men seem to find it much harder than women to make new friends and form close buddy relationships, especially once they stop working. We have found that many women have an easier time in retirement and are not as unhappy or lonely when their spouse dies as men are when they lose their wives. Men—you have got to force yourselves to forge new platonic relationships with other men and with women, especially if you plan a long life. Bond over sports, cards, cars, wine, or whatever. Meet people at groups that cater to your interest. Become a "regular" at the local coffee shop, or volunteer someplace where your skills come in handy. If you are open, interested in others, and friendly, of course, you can't help but meet and make new friends.

SPEND QUALITY TIME WITH YOUR GRANDCHILDREN

If you are lucky enough to have grandchildren, you can experience an enormous amount of joy in getting to know them and watching them mature. If not, and you want children in your life, you can involve yourself with friends' grandchildren or young nieces and nephews, or involve yourself with children's charities. We know one woman, who never married and has no children, who, despite these facts, loves children. She volunteers tirelessly at a shelter and day care for at-risk women and children. She has developed many mentoring, close relationships with children, many of whom she has seen grow up, go to college, and enter the workforce as successful people.

■ **Make it a priority to see your grandchildren regularly.** Research shows 56 percent of grandparents see one of their grandchildren at least once a week, and 60 percent of them babysit regularly.
■ **Spend some one-on-one time with each grandchild**—whether it's in person, by e-mail, or on the telephone. Make each one of them feel special.

■ **Find hobbies or activities you can enjoy together.** Do an art project, start a stamp collection, enjoy a sport, scrapbook or bake cookies together. Whatever it is, find a common interest. Do things that have meaning to just the two of you.

■ **Take trips.** Consider taking each grandchild on a "just the two (or three if you're including your mate) of us" vacation for a few hours or a few days, whatever works for you, when he or she is around age ten or there is a major event in their lives, such as a birthday or a graduation. You can go to the top of the Eiffel Tower or picnic by a river. It's not where you are but the quality of the time you're spending together. During an outing or any time you're together, remember to listen to, not talk *at*, your grandchild— or any child, for that matter. It makes for a delightful conversation and lifelong bonding.

■ **Adopt a pet.** Depending on your relationship with it, a pet may fall in your inner circle, not on the peripheral ring. An animal's unconditional love offers tremendous camaraderie. Some people have pets as an alternative to children, or as a substitute for or in addition to children, grandchildren, or close friends. Pets can give you a reason to greet the day—they provide a sense of responsibility, an exercise program, and a great opening for social interchange during walks with other pet owners.

Domestic animals are more popular than they have ever been before in the United States, and are at the top of many people's must-have list—just look at all the designer products and services that mimic our own needs and excesses. Here's what one of our survey respondents had to say on the importance of pets in her life:

I never wanted to have children. My life has been full without them. I have a wonderful mate, a career that I love, travel and fulfilling life experiences. I am lucky enough to have nieces and nephews that I am very close to and involved with; it must feel something like having grandchildren. I love being with them, but I don't have to raise them. My "child" is my dog. Besides my husband, of all the things that I've had and done, my one constant love is my dog. I can't imagine my life without her. She's there for me and I am there for her.

—RETIREMENT DOCS' SURVEY

YOUR INTERMEDIATE AND OUTER CIRCLES

When we retire, our social world usually narrows. We don't have the everyday relationships we once had at work, and we may find that we spend more time focused on our family and other members in our inner circle. Keeping a network of friends in our intermediate and outer circles can keep our perspective broadening and our interests expanding. Maybe you have a friend who shares your passion for the opera or basketball and you decide to get season tickets together? Or another friend introduced you to French films and now you're hooked.

- **Plan ahead.** Research shows group interaction decreases as we age. Start and maintain your new and ongoing relationships as much as possible in your retirement's phase one's planning for retirement, and phase two's semiretirement.
- **Be willing to take the time to develop new friendships and maintain current ones.** For many of us, this takes a recognized and planned effort on our parts: Don't skip that poker game or book club just because you've settled in. Get out of the house and off to that garden show. "It's raining," you say? Get an umbrella! All of those other people managed to get there.
- **Have a number of single friends.** When we're married, most of our friends tend to be involved in—we've all heard it many times—"a couple's world." Should you lose your spouse, you'll have a base of friends who won't have the time commitment that a partnership requires.

■ **If necessary, reeducate yourself: Make new friends.** Ask other people for input, make a list, read the local newspaper. Find things that are interesting to you and go there. Do you love to read? Volunteer for a couple of hours a week at your local library. Socialize in churches, hobby groups, volunteer groups, or schools, or take your dog to a local dog park; play cards, start going to the local ball games, join an exercise class; the list is endless. Involve yourself with a group of people who enjoy your hobby. Remember, friendships usually start via a common interest and over time develop by openly sharing thoughts, interests, and concerns. The key is not the activity; it's how you develop and use the activity as an opportunity to expand your support group.

■ **Get online.** An area of marked expansion for continuing senior social interaction has been the Internet. SeniorNet.com has led this movement along with many other dotcoms. The computer has given isolated retirees the opportunity to communicate with friends and potential friends, plus the ability to exchange information in a world of available and interesting topics, all the while providing excellent mental stimulation.

E-Friends

MySpace and Facebook, while not specifically geared to Baby Boomers (Facebook started as a site for college students), are welcoming to them. Both of these sites make it easy to create a page and connect with others who share your interests. In addition, a national organization called meetup.com helps people organize local, in-person meetings for all sorts of things—from singles events to garden clubs. It's a fantastic way to connect with people in your area who share your interest. Here is a list of some other online social networking Web sites, with their taglines, that are geared to Baby Boomers and their concerns.

(continued)

www.eons.com—Lovin' life: the flip side of 50

www.BOOMj.com—Boomer Nation Lifestyle Network

www.reZOOM.com—Redefining life for an ageless generation

www.BoomerTowne.com

www.BoomerGirl.com—Welcome to the Club

www.eldr.com—Celebrating aging

www.RedwoodAge.com—Think. Share. Act. Live.

www.BoomSpeak.com—Your whole life's in front of you

www.eGenerations.com—Connect. Learn. Explore.

www.itsBoomerTime.com—Having fun . . . while changing the
world

www.GrowingBolder.com—The Revolution Is Coming Soon

www.Boomer-Living.com— . . . Enhancing the lives of Active Baby
Boomers

www.tbd.com (TeeBeeDee)—Sharing Experiences to Thrive

www.LifeTwo.com— . . . Midlife Improvement

www.MyBoomerPlace.com—Like MySpace, but better . . . for
people over 40

www.MyPrimetime.com—Personal Trainer for Life

www.secondprime.com—Where people 50+ connect, create, and
contribute

www.MapleandLeek.com (United Kingdom)—Live it up at 50+.
Adventures start here

www.GrownUps.co.nz (New Zealand)—50+ Community

STAY INVOLVED WITH YOUR PERIPHERAL CIRCLE

There are a number of people who may not be your close friends or colleagues, but who are crucial to your well-being and "life management."

- **Know who they are.** In your second career, this circle is made up of the people who are necessary for keeping your life in order and functioning smoothly—people like your doctor, your accountant, your attorney, your banker, your insurance agent, your pastor, and anyone else you can think of who provides you with services you rely on. Both you and your spouse should become well acquainted with these professionals. If, and when, something happens to one of you, it will allow the other to feel comfortable continuing on with the business at hand.

- **Make sure you are responsible for something living to tend to.** For example, a plant, a garden, an animal, a bunch of pigeons, or a pool of koi all give you a reason to get up in the morning, for without you your charges may not exist. Caregiving and caretaking are important to your overall well-being.

It is never, ever too late to make new friends. Make widening your social circle a top priority now if you feel that your circle will dwindle significantly once you fully retire. Friends who share your interests in sports, hobbies, crafts, or specific subjects will make wonderful companions when you begin pursuing leisure activities and passions, the two topics we discuss next.

7

TRAIT FIVE: KICK BACK—
ENJOY LEISURE TIME

There is nothing more remarkable in the life of Socrates than that he found time in his old age to learn to dance and play on instruments and thought it was time well spent.

—MONTAIGNE, RENAISSANCE SCHOLAR

Retirement, for many of us, represents the first time in our lives when we are accountable only to ourselves. Our working lives probably left many of us with little room for personal leisure. Then one day we finally have time to transfer our energy from earning a living to the business of living life. It's exchanging a paycheck for a payoff both in pleasure and retirement satisfaction. When all that time hits us in the face, we often become consumed with our newfound freedom, and the activities and projects we've had on the back burner for years finally come to life. Life is exciting! We accomplish our goals in the first six to twelve months of our retirement, and then we're left wondering: What in the world am I going to do with all that free time?

To have a successful retirement, people need to begin the process of discovery again. Though now as I face it, I wonder, is it possible to live a meaningful, fulfilled life if work is no longer the center of it?

—RETIREMENT DOCS' SURVEY

It seems to me that most of my life was spent living for tomorrow. In my retirement, I am living for today. I find I want fewer and fewer material possessions and more and more experiences.

—RETIREMENT DOCS' SURVEY

The answer to that question is found in phase one, before you retire. You should be cultivating as many leisure activities as you can at that time. As we've already explained, transitioning from work to retirement leisure will be easier for you if you have certain behaviors in place before you leave your job. Bear in mind that a partiality to certain leisure activities is usually not developed on short notice. For example, an interest in literature or appreciation for classical music usually takes many years to develop. It's also a good idea to develop and include a number of less-demanding interests and activities years before you are forced by age or physical limitations to do so.

If you're saying to yourself, "I've been too busy working to cultivate a lot of outside interests," don't also think it's too late to do anything about it. Everyone has at least one or two activities or areas that they are interested in, apart from (or even related to) the work they do. Whether you are about to retire, have just retired, or have been retired for a while, now is the time to start cultivating your interests and researching ways to get involved in them. You can begin developing interests by making a list of things you enjoy doing or think you would, could, or might enjoy (we give you plenty of opportunities to do so in this book). Even the act of *researching* an activity, *planning* a trip, *organizing* an outing, or *reading up* on a particular topic are in themselves ways to develop an interest.

Walter Kerr, author of *The Decline of Pleasure,* points out: "The twentieth century has relieved us of much labor without, at the same time, relieving us of the conviction that only labor is meaningful."

Our survey respondents were asked to rate their success as well as their partners' (if applicable), in developing and achieving satisfying leisure activities. We weren't surprised to find that our highly successful retirees had much commonality and positive support going for them. Couples felt that there was equal and adequate intellectual stimulation for them both, that they had ample social activities they did alone and together, and that each partner was or had been involved in planning and preparing for their retirement. Our respondents also said they watched television together 50 percent of the time, and surprise—they shared equally in handling the remote.

And, *aaah,* television and our dedication to it. Surveys show that just about 40 percent of our leisure time is spent watching TV. It is by far the number-one leisure activity from phase one right on through phase four, with viewing time increasing significantly as we age.

> *My wife is always after me to "turn that thing off and do something productive."*
> *She's an avid reader, and I've asked her what she thinks is the difference between*
> *watching programs that are interesting to me, and reading for hours on end the*
> *books she thinks are interesting. So far she hasn't answered. Maybe she's busy*
> *reading!*
>
> —RETIREMENT DOCS' SURVEY

There is no question that television watching can be intellectually stimulating, and watching sporting events or a thriller can increase your heart rate. TV is relaxing, and if you do live alone, it can provide a sense of "company." Our concern is moderation. Reclining in front of the tube five and a half hours a day, day in and day out, is the norm for many viewers over age sixty. That's excessive. Examine your viewing habits and make sure you're not glued in one place for far too long. And if you are going to stay tuned to television, at least come up with a few multitasking efforts during some of those viewing hours—knitting, crocheting, needlepoint, crosswords (during commercial breaks), organizing photos, etcetera.

This leads us to the key concept in spending free time well—leisure *doesn't* mean idleness. Controlled trials prove that mental and physical workouts, in the context of leisure activities, are major factors in keeping your mind alert and functioning. The best kind of leisure activities not only keep you entertained but also relax you, help you enjoy friends and family, and even connect you to potential passions and purposes (which we discuss in the next chapter). The great characteristic of leisure is that it does not need to be

Important with a capital *I*, or Meaningful with a capital *M*. Consequential activities are important. But in order to have a balanced life it is necessary to spend some of your time doing things simply because they are fun and not because they are vitally important to the greater significance of your life.

> *I retired at sixty and was very active. I golfed nearly every day. By seventy-six, medical problems and the loss of my wonderful wife took the wind out of my sails. But never count yourself finished until you are. At a class reunion, a chance meeting with a "girl" I hadn't seen for years led to my second marriage. I'm now eighty-four, don't golf anymore, but once or twice a week we get together with a group of friends and have savage putting competitions. We take great strolls, go on outings identifying and counting birds for our local Audubon Society, and in general enjoy life. I am much happier today than I have been in a long time.*
>
> —RETIREMENT DOCS' SURVEY

Leisure is about pleasure and unwinding: taking in a ridiculous but hilarious new comedy, reading a trashy espionage novel that you simply cannot put down, relaxing out on the deck with a really cold beer and a really good buddy, checking out fishing rods at the sporting goods store, or poking around antique shops on a Sunday afternoon. Or leisure can involve more physical projects, especially those long overdue, like renovating the bathroom, building a patio, or organizing the basement or closet (notice how enjoyable those things can be when you actually have time to do them?).

> *I don't like structure in retirement. I like going with the flow, though I have many interests, including my family, physical exercise (mainly running long distances, cross-country biking, and strenuous swimming), flying airplanes, golfing, reading, and gardening. While I make few plans in the main, when I wake up, depending on the weather, I will do two or three different activities that day. I randomly rotate them on a day-to-day basis. The core activity, however, is a daily hour to an hour and a half of one of my exercises. My goal is elevating my heart rate.*
>
> —RETIREMENT DOCS' SURVEY

A work ethic can be deeply ingrained in our psyches, and for many good reasons: It gives us an identity, self-esteem, and a psychological high for a job well done. This is why for many people, the perfect leisure activity is part-time employment, especially if it's of your own choosing, it's at your own pace, it isn't stressful, and it enhances your personal satisfaction. If your decision to "work till you drop" allows you to be of productive value to your employer and yourself—go for it. Just make sure you're not being a hanger-on. You need to continue to contribute wherever and however you find yourself involved.

It doesn't require a Herculean effort to begin shifting your perspective about yourself. Read your local newspaper events calendar. It will supply you with myriad interesting activities. That's just what we did and found listed, to name just a few, a model railroad club, square dancing with instructions, Meals on Wheels, a quilt guild, a toastmasters club, a runner's run (all abilities and ages welcome), a genealogical society meeting, an Apple computer users group meeting, an invitation to become involved in a food bank, a request for volunteer readers in area grade schools, an acting workshop, and a golf tournament. These all appeared on one page! As we mentioned in the support groups section, meetup.com is an online resource for meetings of all kinds of groups, including those interested in specific leisure pursuits. Your neighborhood may also have a block association with an online component that you can check for upcoming events.

I am a planner. I started field-testing various leisure activities ten years before my retirement. I made specific plans to use them if I became physically infirm as well as for the normal aging changes that would occur. I worked on developing activities I could do alone and with my mate, our friends, and my friends. I stopped working full-time seven years ago, but I have a work ethic mentality; that is, I have a need to stay productive. But I'm getting much better as time passes, and I feel that I've got my dilemmas under control. As I get older, my leisure activities are becoming more and more family-oriented. These are the best years of my life in large part because of a strong support group. For the first time in my adult life, I feel that I am in control of my time.

—DR. FRITZ

I've had so many outside interests in my life, other than medicine, that when I was forced to limit my surgery practice because of some visual problems, I hit the ground running. My strong family support group and wide circle of friends frequently allow just the two of us, my wife and me, only a few nights a week relaxing at home. While we value our time together, we also feel fortunate to have such a wide circle of support, and look forward to the stimulation that comes from our outings, be they with family, friends, or a new adventure. Since childhood, I have had so many interests, hobbies, and activities that I never feel that I have enough time for all of them.

I love sports, was a high school team player, loved working with my hands, and have always been in love with the arts. I have taken fine woodworking courses from some of the top craftsmen in our country. It's not that I wanted to be the world's best woodworker. Rather, I wanted to learn their techniques and enjoy their expertise. In fact, I'm just going to meet with a very talented guy who's going to teach me how to carve decoys. I guess I fell into the select group that had practiced the "retirement hop" without much conscious awareness of planning or preparation. However, as time goes on, I am working, as is Dr. Fritz, to fine-tune my eight traits. I feel that what lies ahead in phases three and four needs planning, particularly for a wide range of age-related fallback leisure activities.

—DR. JIM

And don't forget to include social support groups. There are card games (look at the popularity of poker and bridge), any kind of hobby club you can think of, book clubs, dinner groups, and rock and roll bands. We just read an article about the resurgence of the musicians among us dusting off those long-neglected instruments and gathering to enjoy some good times, jamming in their garages—and most of the participants were sixty or older!

I spent close to forty years doing the same work. My life was full of good fortune. I have an occupation that kept me, for the main part, fully engaged. I have a wife, children, and grandchildren who currently keep me balanced and on my toes. I have lots of friends, though I must admit that the majority of them were coworkers, and that part of my life has taken the biggest adjusting to. But I'm lucky—

the family grew up and my extended family is now a big part of where I look forward to spending my time. And though I miss the day-to-day structure and interaction of what I did for so long, I also now have the time to devote to my love of hiking and all the planning it involves. I recently began studying cartology, and that's opened up a whole new interest for me. I have plenty of family and friends (and some new hiking boots) who remain fit, able, and ready to go see the world.

—RETIREMENT DOCS' SURVEY

DIAGNOSIS

To find out if there are enough leisure activities in your life, answer the following questions. Don't hesitate to duplicate some activities within different categories. To get you thinking, how about golf, tennis, walking, bird-watching, gardening, family events, being with your grandchildren, cultural events, arts, movies, plays, reading, writing, painting, volunteering, elder hostels, community college classes, and church involvement? The sky's the limit. A keen interest in a specific hobby often creates an expert mentality and a feeling of accomplishment, but keep in mind the importance of having a variety of leisure activities. The point of these activities is to stimulate but also free your mind. Factor in activities that can be done when health problems, caregiving responsibilities, a change in economics, or age limitations occur.

Make sure you've included intellectual motivation and physical challenges in each of the categories below. They generate a sense of accomplishment and well-being. Just as muscles and bones remain healthy when exercised, our minds stay healthy when challenged. Remember, the more you can list, the better off you'll be.

■ List ten or more leisure activities that you do with your mate or mutual friends. For example, travel, play cards, golf, garden, go to the theater, volunteer, spend time with grandchildren and other family, and join various organizations—social, political, or spiritual. If there is a particular activity that you are deeply immersed in and it has several parts, it can count as three. For example, gardening could potentially count as planting, learning about horticulture, and caring for the landscape, and maybe even organizing the local garden club.

1. We enjoy . . .
2. We enjoy . . .
3. We enjoy . . .
4. We enjoy . . .
5. We enjoy . . .
6. We enjoy . . .
7. We enjoy . . .
8. We enjoy . . .
9. We enjoy . . .
10. We enjoy . . .

■ List ten or more leisure activities that you enjoy doing by yourself or with your own personal friends. Some examples are golf, tennis, attending sports events, exercising, reading, watching television, card games, gardening, social clubs, fishing, listening to music, visiting old friends, genealogy, woodworking, and spending time with grandchildren. As above, any multipart activity can count as more than one on the list.

1. I enjoy . . .
2. I enjoy . . .
3. I enjoy . . .
4. I enjoy . . .
5. I enjoy . . .
6. I enjoy . . .
7. I enjoy . . .
8. I enjoy . . .
9. I enjoy . . .
10. I enjoy . . .

▪ List ten or more activities that make you feel good about yourself, things that make you feel as if you're helping others, affirming that you're still a player, or that there is a reason you are on this earth. Some examples are volunteering, writing, managing assets, teaching, lecturing, part-time employment, civic groups, and belonging to various local and national organizations. As above, any multipart activity can count as more than one on the list.

1. I am involved in . . .
2. I am involved in . . .
3. I am involved in . . .
4. I am involved in . . .
5. I am involved in . . .
6. I am involved in . . .
7. I am involved in . . .
8. I am involved in . . .
9. I am involved in . . .
10. I am involved in . . .

Both of us intend to be in phase two for as long as we're physically and mentally able to. We enjoy consulting with patients, speaking, writing, and doing research. This ongoing work gives us a feeling of self-worth and softens the loss of identity and self-esteem we received when practicing full-time medicine.

—JIM AND FRITZ, THE RETIREMENT DOCS

THE RETIREMENT DOCS' LEISURE PRESCRIPTION

When faced with excess time, the vast majority of retirees continue doing the same activities they did before their retirement, but they expand the amount of time they give to them. Our highly successful retirees were all expanders. They added to or field-tested relationships and involvement with new friends, hobbies, and activities to see which ones they wanted to pursue over the long term. Optimally, the process of planning and field-testing for filling in free time begins at least five to ten years *before* retirement, but very few of us are going to find ourselves in that position. Remember, several years before you retire, when you are retiring, or if you've been retired for some time, it's never too late to begin making a plan for good use of your leisure time. Just make sure it's a pleasure putting that plan into place!

To make good use of leisure time, keep these things in mind:

- Spend time with vibrant, stimulating, upbeat, and optimistic people.
- Increase activities, reading materials, and viewing materials that create positive feelings. Decrease those that create negative feelings.
- Include mental stimulation, physical exertion, and social contact throughout the four phases of your retirement.
- Select some interests that make you feel a sense of responsibility and give you a feeling of self-respect.
- Contribute to the well-being of other people.
- If retirement doesn't work, "un-retire." Full- or part-time employment is a great idea if it's enjoyable.
- The best leisure activities promote a healthy lifestyle.
- Look for ways to add spice to your life. Take risks and try new adventures.
- Retirement gives you the freedom to do what you want to do. Enjoy and protect it.
- The spirit of a leisure-time interest is as important as the activity. Eliminate anything mentally stressful, and spend your leisure time leisurely!
- Ideal leisure includes educational activities.
- Increase your social networking. Become involved in a variety of leisure activities that include people of all ages.
- Reach out and make your life meaningful. It usually won't happen unless you make the effort.

Success or failure in our second career will in great part be measured in terms of how we use or abuse the leisure time we have. The writer Freya Stark put it beautifully when she wrote something we can all think about, whatever our age and whatever our abilities:

> On the whole, age comes more gently to those who have some doorway into the abstract world—art or philosophy or learning—regions where the years are scarcely noticed and the young and the old can meet in a pale, truthful light.

Finally, we want you to remember that leisure is about pleasure. There is no better time to indulge in fun. Think of retirement as a sabbatical—this is the "someday" you've talked about for years, as in "Someday, I'm going to learn to sail, perfect the tango, or read *Moby-Dick*." The time has arrived—seize the day!

8

TRAIT SIX: HERE'S TO YOUR HEALTH

In health there is freedom. Health is the first of all liberties.
—HENRI-FRÉDÉRIC AMIEL, SWISS WRITER

Retirement Docs' Survey respondents rated a healthy lifestyle second most important after planning. Even so, we decided to name it trait six because we feel strongly that the psychological components of retirement are too often overlooked, and therefore more crucial to concentrate on first. Still, physical well-being is essential for a successful retirement, and our most highly successful retirees were also the most fit and active. In fact, these happy, healthy retirees are so dedicated to keeping fit and well that they consider exercise and healthy eating *nonnegotiable passions.* They know that the payoff for taking care of their bodies is increased energy, a better mood, and a greater overall satisfaction with life.

Clearly, given the choice (and you are given a choice), achieving and maintaining the best health we can is a real advantage to living longer and better. Can you remember how old you were when you realized that you and you alone, not your mother, spouse, or doctor, were responsible for your health and well-being? Years ago when we were in medical school, we were taught that a person's allotted lifetime, barring an untimely accidental death, was based heavily on genetic makeup. The conventional wisdom (which 70 percent of our respondents still believe) was that some of us were lucky with our ancestral pipelines, and some weren't. But now we know better. As the saying goes, it's not so much the cards you've been dealt but how you play them. We take that idea a step further: after age sixty, it's not so much about the genes you have been dealt, but it's how much help you're willing to give them.

Once you reach sixty, you have even more control of your health, your life satisfaction, and, to a great extent, your longevity than you did when you were younger. Michael F. Roizen, M.D., points out in *Real Age* that, "inherited genetics account for less than 30 percent of all aging effects, and the importance of genetic inheritance matters less and less the older your calendar age. By the age of eighty, behavioral choices account almost entirely for a person's overall health and longevity."

Of course, it's true that there is an occasional blip on the screen—we all know one or two people who seem to defy the odds by some genetically gifted providence, and go for decades abusing their bodies and living to see a healthy ninety-plus years. Think about Bette Davis turning up to spar with David Letterman, puffing away on a cancer stick well into her seventies. We've just celebrated one of our friend's century marks, which she greeted with martini and cigarette in hand. *However, be aware that this is far from the norm.* An article in that highly esteemed bible of medicine *The New England Journal of Medicine* stated that, "not only do persons with better health habits survive longer, but in such persons, disability is postponed and compressed into much fewer years at the end of life." And according to the World Health Organization, "Health isn't the absence of illness, but a presence of well-being, including your physical, mental and social wellness."

> As we age, good health requires the full participation of the individual. I take care of myself because I know that I am my own responsibility. My best doctors are a balanced diet, regular exercise, mental stimulation, and moderation in diet.
>
> —RETIREMENT DOCS' SURVEY

What follows is a rundown of the most important components of good health. We won't insult your intelligence by telling you that maintaining a healthy lifestyle is easy or can be done overnight, especially if you have not been paying attention to certain aspects of your health for a while. No matter—with a few small steps at a time (cutting out fried and processed foods, increasing the amount of vegetables and other whole foods you eat, talking a daily walk, etcetera), you can actually make very big health strides.

DIET AND WEIGHT:
BALANCING THE SCALES

As much as any lifestyle characteristic, excess weight affects health and happiness. Today, more than at any time in our history, Americans are collectively fatter than ever. Our national obesity rates in the United States have doubled since 1980, and 25 percent of our population is obese compared to 7 percent of Europeans.

Excess weight can cause major cardiovascular problems, increased blood pressure, diabetes, and bone and joint problems, as well as an increased incidence of cancer and gout. The list goes on and on. The National Institutes of Health Consensus Development Conference states that in terms of suffering, the psychological burden of obesity alone may be its greatest adverse effect. It is estimated that obesity-related morbidity may account for almost 7 percent of the total health-care costs in the United States. A woman of average height (5 feet 6 inches) with a waistline measuring more than 36 inches has a dramatically increased chance of suffering a heart attack. The same is true for a man of average height (5 feet 10 inches) with a waistline of more than 40 inches.

Your Body Mass Index (BMI) is a fairly new term: it's the measurement of choice for many physicians and researchers when studying obesity. It's also the most accurate way to determine whether you have too few or too many pounds that could translate into health risks.

To calculate an adult BMI, use the following formula (alternatively, use one of the many easy BMI calculators available free on the Internet—use the keywords "BMI calculator" to find one).

- Multiply your weight in pounds by 703.
- Divide that number by your height in inches, squared (e.g., if you're 5'5", that's 65 inches. Your height squared—65 × 65—is 4225).
- Round the first decimal point up if necessary. That is your BMI.

BMI Categories

- Underweight   = 18.5
- Normal weight = 18.5–24.9
- Overweight   = 25–29.9
- Obesity   = 30 or higher

There are numerous Web sites that offer the BMI calculator. We used the National Heart, Lung, and Blood Institute site at www.NHLBISUPPORT .com. If you use the same organization, you'll find the Body Mass Index Calculator listed under Health Associated Tools. This NHLB site has an amazing array of health-related information. What a find! But back to our weight-related info.

What's your BMI? Get it into the normal weight category and positively below 30. Do your part to insure a healthy lifestyle.

A healthy diet and an ideal body weight may provide you with the health base that you need to add to a statistical life expectancy. On the other hand, the markedly obese, besides having weight-related aches and pains, could find themselves decreasing their lifespan by years. In extreme situations, there may be a swing either way of twenty-plus years. Healthy, you might give yourself another twenty-plus. Heavy, you could see a minus-twenty. Significant numbers, don't you think?

UCLA researchers reviewed thirty-one weight-loss studies and concluded that diet programs did not keep the pounds off. It's true that most people initially lose weight, but between a third and two-thirds of dieters regain that weight over a two- to five-year follow-up period. That's probably because in the past decade we have doubled or tripled our portion sizes. Recent research shows that almost 70 percent of us eat everything that we're served—and we get served huge portions at home and in restaurants. Men are three times more likely to eat everything on their plates than are women. A recent article in the *Journal of the American Medical Association* noted that decreasing serving portions by 20 percent extends your life. "Lick the platter clean" is history.

The National Weight Control Registry suggests that the best ways to keep lost pounds off are:

Eat breakfast. The morning meal does not have to be large, but you do need to eat it. A slice of whole-wheat toast with peanut butter or a cup of nonfat yogurt with fruit is enough to get your engine running.

Eat moderately and know what you're eating. Fill your plate with fiber-rich foods like whole grains (brown rice, cracked wheat), beans, deeply colored vegetables (leafy greens, sweet potatoes, tomatoes, carrots, beets), and fruit. Stay away from saturated fat (butter, steak) and stick to "good" fats, such as olive and canola oils, but use them in moderation. Eat lean protein (chicken breast, turkey, egg whites) but in moderation. Three-quarters of your plate should be filled with plant-based foods.

Weigh yourself daily or at least weekly. Make a chart and write down the date and your weight. If you're on a weight-loss program, keep a food journal and write down everything you eat. A free, easy-to-use online example is www.calorie-count.com.

Move everyday—at least thirty to sixty minutes.

Bonus tip: Drink wine and eat chocolate. We now believe that one or two glasses of red wine and a one-inch square of dark chocolate consumed each day may add to longevity and good health.

And one more—on us: Don't eat after dinner.

I'm at the age where food has taken the place of sex in my life. In fact, I've just had a mirror put over my kitchen table.

—RODNEY DANGERFIELD

What Mr. Dangerfield has to say about aging and eating is amusing. Should you find that you've gone ahead and installed the kitchen mirror, use it to take a good look at yourself! Think healthy, look healthy = be healthy.

Meditate on It

Meditation is good for your health. Meditation is simply the practice of sitting comfortably, with eyes closed, for fifteen to twenty minutes twice a day while mentally repeating a simple word or mantra (which can be anything from "yes" to "love"). This practice has drastically reduced medical costs in people aged sixty-five and over, according to a Canadian study. One hundred and sixty-three senior citizens from Quebec reduced visits to physicians by 70 percent during the five-year period after they started to meditate.

Om!

EXERCISE: THE REWARDS OF SWEAT EQUITY

Please note: When exercising, overdoing or pushing too hard, particularly as we get older, is a problem waiting to happen. Before starting any exercise program, consult with your doctor or health-care provider. Begin with something simple that you enjoy (you will never stick with something that you don't like doing), such as walking or riding a bike.

Getting your blood flowing improves your cardiovascular system and increases your lung capacity, your body's two most important systems. At the same time it's elevating your mood and aiding in your longevity. We have a good friend who is famous for shooting his age in most of his golf rounds. He claims his game is so good and so consistent because he never misses a ten-minute morning stretching routine and most days, an hour workout. By the way, he's eighty-four and a newlywed. A recent study by Dr. Teresa Seeman, professor of medicine and epidemiology at UCLA, found seventy- to ninety-year-olds functioned best and had the least psychological stress when they exercised regularly.

Further geriatric research indicates that it's a given—a diverse exercise program improves your perception of your health and aging. An ongoing, ever-adjusting variety of physical activities is ideal throughout the four phases of retirement. Consider walking with a group (keep the pace as fast as you can); joining a bird-watching club where participants go out seasonally on hikes and walks to count bird species; signing up for tap, line, square, or ballroom dancing; going for a hike; playing doubles tennis or golf; or anything that gets you up and out.

Exercise has always been important to me. I was able to transition from running marathons in my thirties to jogging several times a week in my sixties. Now that I'm in my eighties I thoroughly enjoy my walking group. Exercise has kept me active and energized for decades.

—RETIREMENT DOCS' SURVEY

We wanted to schedule a time to interview a friend of ours for this book. He's a psychiatrist who happens to be ninety-six. His receptionist said she would give him our message, adding, "As you know, he's in the office twice a week. Right now he's out with his personal trainer. I know about the book you two are working on, and it seems relevant that you know the doctor works out daily and meets with his trainer three times each week. He's remarkable." The fact that our friend's meetings with his trainer took precedence over the one we hoped to schedule was a good thing.

It's very hard to exercise alone, especially when you are just starting out! If you must, however, most cable television now offers a myriad of exercise programs, and one or two networks are devoted to fitness 24/7.

Based on one's ability, capability, and personality, individual exercise programs vary greatly throughout retirement's four phases. But continued consistency is paramount for overall health and feelings of well-being. This doesn't mean, mentioned earlier, that it's necessary to have a personal trainer or to attend an exercise class, though either is a smart choice, especially for someone who is getting back into exercise or embarking on a program for the first time. A certified fitness professional can help motivate you, and he or she can help you design, stick to, and implement the right program. The YMCA has personal trainers on staff, and membership is very affordable, especially for those who meet certain age requirements. Certified trainers are able to teach you to exercise properly for maximum benefit and minimum injury, and you meet other likeminded people at the gym.

Weight-bearing exercises are essential for bone strength and flexibility. According to a recent AARP study, people eighty and older who lifted weights were from 58 to 74 percent more optimistic than were people who didn't pump iron! Nothing fancy is required, but consistency is. If you miss a day, get back at it. One guy we know was twenty-four when he spotted a fifteen-pound steel rod in a trash bin. He's used it as his exercise weight daily for the past forty-four years.

People who think they have no time for exercise will sooner or later have more than enough time for illness

—JIM AND FRITZ, THE RETIREMENT DOCS

And for you "naysaying, just-won't-do-it" non-exercisers, please remember that even thirty minutes three times a week has obvious benefits if it gets your heart rate up. We once read that it takes twenty-eight days to make something a habit and three days to undo it. Exercise as you live: take the stairs instead of the elevator, garden, and park as far from the grocery store as you can to add additional steps to your day. Or grab a friend and commit to meeting three times a week for a power walk around the neighborhood. Making a commitment to another person makes us do what we should do, rather than thinking about what we should do and then not quite getting around to it. One woman we know took a daily walk with a friend who lived next door. It became a much-looked-forward-to evening ritual. It was "me time" for both of them, a time to unwind, review the day, and get some exercise.

A LAUGHING MATTER

Snicker, giggle, chuckle, and laugh until your sides hurt! Laughter is another important component of a healthy lifestyle. William Fry, M.D., professor of psychiatry at Stanford University Medical School, found that while kindergarten-aged children laugh about three hundred times a day, adults laugh only about seventeen times per day. Maybe we are growing older because we stop laughing! In an article by *Oregonian* columnist Margie Boulé, medical researchers specializing in laughter and the effect it has on our well-being found that laughing lowers blood pressure, reduces weight, strengthens hearts, boosts immune systems, and lowers stress hormones, and those are just some of the benefits.

Indeed, doctors all over the world are studying the effects of laughter on the immune and cardiovascular systems and finding amazing results. There is a now a field of medical study actually called "laughter therapy," which is designed to study the potential for laughter to promote healing and overall well-being. For instance, researchers at the UCLA Neuropsychiatric Research Institute and Hospital showed that patients undergoing painful medical procedures had significantly better pain tolerance while laughing at comedy shows during their private, individual procedures. The treatments went by faster for these patients, and they felt less afraid and less stressed. Dr. Jim's "doctor, heal thyself" prescription while recovering from recent major surgery was a daily dose of the Comedy Channel. He's fully recovered and, in part, found that laughter was indeed "the best medicine."

Medications: Too Easy to Swallow

Americans may well be the most overmedicated people in the world. Whether it's prescription medicine, over-the-counter drugs, or herbal products, many of us take too many medications. It seems to be our mentality that we should have something to take for each and every ailment we suffer, when the truth is that the tincture of time is most often the best cure for minor ailments. Do you realize that 98 percent of the time the potential interaction among any three medications that we may be ingesting is probably unknown?

Our highly successful retirees, with an average age of sixty-eight, while healthy, still take an average daily dose of two prescription drugs, two over-the-counter medications (such as vitamins, aspirin, and decongestants), and 0.5 herbal products. That adds up to a minimum of 4.5 pills a day, which is still about *half* the national average for sixty-eight-year-olds. That's a lot of swallowing. Women take more medications than men until age seventy, at which time men and women take the same amount. It's in your best interest to reevaluate many herbal and over-the-counter drugs. Herbal products often have significant variability in their ingredients and potency, as well as unknown interactions with other drugs.

While the exact content and potency are uniform in over-the-counter drugs, they are often used in excess and may interfere with prescription medication. Know what you are taking and why. Ask your physician if you can decrease the number and dosage of your prescription drugs. Data shows that the more "doctor-hopping" a person does, the more prescription medication he or she will take—and the more risk of combining drugs that should not be taken together.

In all probability, most of us are at least 40 percent overmedicated.

—BRITISH JOURNAL OF GENERAL PRACTICE

THE SMOKING GUN: CIGARETTES

I kicked most all of my bad habits by myself, but I needed professional help to stop smoking.

—RETIREMENT DOCS' SURVEY

The four leading causes of death in America are

- Heart disease
- Cancer
- Stroke
- Chronic obstructive pulmonary disease, including varying combinations of chronic bronchitis, asthma, and emphysema.

Half of all long-term smokers will face a severe—that's right, *severe*—form of one of these four diseases. However, if you're a smoker and can stop, quitting has shown a decrease in the incidence of tobacco-related diseases in as short a time as five months.

Here are some statistics that might make any of you smokers want to rethink lighting up. And those of you inhaling anyone else's smoke—change locations.

- Smoking from one to fourteen cigarettes daily will statistically decrease a life span by three years.
- Smokers lighting up fifteen to twenty-four cigarettes each day can subtract five years from their life expectancy.
- Smoke twenty-five or more cigarettes a day and expect to die eight years earlier than a nonsmoker.

And we haven't begun to talk about the decreased quality of life that smoking causes!

As for secondhand smoke:

■ Secondhand smoke inhaled one hour per day decreases life expectancy by a year.

■ One to three hours per day of direct exposure to secondhand smoke reduces life expectancy by two years.

■ More than three hours per day of secondhand smoke inhalation shortens a life span by three years.

This is heavy statistical data. It is our hope that our children and their children will educate themselves regarding the perils of tobacco and then pass it on, snuffing this killer out for good.

THE SOBERING FACTS ABOUT ALCOHOL

There are love songs about its magic. We use it to toast special occasions, and there are pilgrimages to see it produced. We marvel at the multitude of beers, fine wines, and well-aged spirits. It relaxes us, it enables us, and it makes our aches and pains feel better. Its power is magical. Or is it? Just like anything that's out of balance with our body's needs, there are some very sobering facts about alcohol use and abuse.

A Gallup Poll survey has asked the same question annually since 1947. It is: "Has alcohol abuse caused problems in your family?" That first year, 15 percent of the respondents answered "yes." Recently it was 29 percent. In an *American Journal of Psychiatry* article, authors George Vaillant and Kenneth Mukamal placed the overuse of alcohol as one of six major predictive factors for overall failure in life. They wrote that "It's not only alcohol's toll on a person's health, but the destructive force it has on the alcohol abuser's support group. . . . The abuse destroys both health and happiness."

Some current literature recommends no more than two drinks of spirits per day for men and one for women. Moderation is the key. If you don't have a drinking problem, that is. If you aren't an alcoholic, there are some benefits from imbibing (there are *no* benefits to drinking for those who cannot control themselves around booze). Drinking alcohol in moderation is associated with an increased life expectancy of a year or more, though the added year isn't realized until a man reaches forty to fifty years old, and until women reach menopause or their late forties or early fifties. One four-ounce glass of wine or a one-ounce drink of spirits (such as gin or Scotch) may ease stress and relax aches and pains. Recent studies show that red wine contains compounds that may protect us from heart disease, diabetes, and even dementia. Plus, there's enjoyment many of us find in a glass of wine or a cocktail that pleasantly signals the end of our day.

Many, if not most, physicians feel that if you've never been a drinker, don't start. The older we get, the slower we metabolize. And our systems give alcohol the green light first, absorbing it into our bloodstream before anything else it happens to enter with. Add those two facts up and adjust accordingly: slower metabolizing and alcohol's digestive dominance.

Statistics show that many retirees consume more alcohol once they stop working. Less time on the job can often, for many reasons, equal more drinking, so that's something to keep in mind.

SNOOZE CONTROL

People who get a good, solid sleep are more alert, healthier, and happier—and even weigh less than those who do not get *at least* seven hours of sleep per night. An average night's sleep in 1910 was nine hours; currently it's less than seven and a half. The National Sleep Foundation and other sleep experts say that adults need anywhere from seven to nine hours of uninterrupted sleep.

Most of our survey respondents thought they got enough sleep, though a small number of them alluded to sleep problems but chose to more or less ignore them. That isn't surprising, since insomnia and sleep disorders can be common in older people. Some of the symptoms mentioned—and there were quite a few—were difficulty falling asleep, waking often, waking too early, an inability to get back to sleep, waking up tired, snoring, unpleasant feelings in the legs, and interrupted breathing (gasping). If you have any of the above symptoms and they are ongoing over a prolonged period of time (a few months or more), get professional help.

Changing sleep habits is preferable to taking pills. Your bedroom should be dedicated to sleeping and relaxing only. (Move the TV into the living room, and don't pay bills lying in bed—talk about nerve-wracking!) Avoid caffeine, alcohol, and extremely spicy meals late at night. Set and maintain regular sleep times. It's a known fact that senior citizens need seven hours per night of uninterrupted sleep.

And napping? If you happen to be a nap-taker, it's one of retirement's great pleasures, and there is good evidence that proves that it's good for you. Statistics have shown that a twenty- to thirty-minute nap every day decreases the incidence of heart attacks. In a good article on napping, *New York Times* reporter Mary Duenwald writes: "What sleep loss damages is thinking ability: learning, memory, concentration, and decision making. . . . The famously smart and productive—Leonardo da Vinci and Albert Einstein amongst them—have been some of the nap's biggest proponents. The director of the Sleep Research Centre at Loughborough University, England, commented, 'Sleep is by the brain and for the brain.' And a recent Harvard School of Public Health Study in Greece found that adults who took siestas at least three times a week for thirty minutes had a lower death rate from heart attacks."

We think Winston Churchill said it best: "Don't think you will be doing less work because you sleep during the day. That's a foolish notion held by people who have no imagination."

Driving: The Force Behind the Course

Driving is independence, it's the American way, and it's our right. We couldn't wait to get behind the wheel, and now we're determined to stay there, whatever our age. It's a fact: car accidents start to increase at age sixty and continue to rise with each decade. AARP offers a driving course for retirees that has decreased accidents so noticeably that most insurance companies give participants 10 to 20 percent percent off its premiums.

That's a terrific incentive because no one wants to give up his or her license or, worse yet, have someone else demand that it be relinquished. Count us among the automobile-able. If we could have our way, we would drive to our own memorial services.

So, out of consideration for all aging drivers, we've written about elderly driving issues in the third person, something for "the others among us" to keep in mind.

- **Eliminate** night driving as soon as failing vision dictates.
- **Avoid** driving during rush hour or to busy locations, if doing so causes a stressful trip. One can choose a less-traveled route during busy times or simply travel at less-crowded times of day (Tuesday and Wednesday afternoons, for example).
- **Protect** the person behind the wheel and others by driving a heavier car with a bright exterior color.
- **Observe and obey driving laws.** Speed limits are there for a reason. Decrease speed if necessary or step on it—driving too slowly causes accidents too. Go with the flow. On highways and freeways, the passing lane is there for that specific reason. How many drivers act as though the fast lane has been created just for them? Pass and return, right is right, and it's the law!
- **Increase** the distance between the operator's car and other vehicles by at least a car length.

MENTAL HEALTH: THINK IT OVER

For my overall mental health, I identify the times that I'm the most content. Then I expand on those times and repeat them as much as possible. On the other hand, I try to identify the times I least enjoy and reduce or eliminate them as much as I can.

—RETIREMENT DOCS' SURVEY

Falling into depression, as we get older, is a real risk. The National Institutes of Health's Institute on Aging reports that severe depressive symptoms occur in about 15 percent of people sixty-five to seventy-nine years old, and in 23 percent of those eighty-five and older, yet often individuals and their family, friends, or primary caregivers don't recognize them. Temporary depression or sadness following a major traumatic event (loss of a job, death of a loved one) is normal. The good news is that the amount of mental stress we live with may not be as important as how we manage it. Depression is one of the most preventable and treatable diseases in all of medicine. If multiple symptoms (see the box opposite for a list) occur and last more than a few weeks, one should suspect major depression and immediately seek out professional counseling, support groups, and/or drug therapy. Current prescription antidepressants can be highly effective. However, it may take some time, in conjunction with your doctor, to find the right drug and the correct dose for you.

Before popping a pill, try some less-invasive techniques to fight the blues. Physical and mental health are closely associated—more than any time in modern medicine, we find the symbiosis between body and mind linked to overall health and happiness. In fact, many of the traits in this book, such as developing a positive attitude, and finding and pursuing a passion, have been shown to be effective weapons against depression. In addition, the "talking cure" and cognitive therapy have both been shown to be effective treatments for depression.

Depression is a biochemical illness, and willpower alone is not always the answer. Since it may not be perceived as "masculine," men don't seek professional treatment as often as women do. This may be in part why older Caucasian males have a 70 percent higher suicide rate than Caucasian women of the same age. Mild forms of memory loss can also become common as we mature. We can't emphasize enough the importance of stimulating your brain. In several controlled clinical trials, doing crossword puzzles, playing cards, and social intellectual interchange delayed brain degeneration. And forgetfulness can increase if we become anxious or experience stress. But keep in mind that misplacing your keys or glasses occasionally is a normal

Classic signs of depression are

- Apathy
- Weight changes
- Appetite changes
- Sleep disturbances
- Sluggishness
- Guilt
- Feelings of worthlessness
- Poor concentration
- Thoughts of death and suicide

part of aging, and though we may feel sensitive or let it upset us, it's not going to go away. We all do it. We have all, at one time or another, entered a room with a specific purpose in mind only to wonder why we're standing there. Memory usually returns under relaxed conditions. In reality, most of us aren't as forgetful as we think we are.

Normal aging does not necessarily result in a significant decline in intelligence, memory or learning ability.
—NANCY HOOYMAN AND H. ASUMAN KIYAK, *SOCIAL GERONTOLOGY*

Tragically, however, for some people memory problems are a sign of dementia, the most common form being Alzheimer's disease. The National Institutes of Health and the drug industry are investing heavily in research into the various forms of this disease, and promising therapies are in the pipeline, but for the moment there are really no effective treatments or preventive medicines on the market.

We don't know why, but women up to age eighty are two to three times more likely to develop Alzheimer's than men. After reaching age eighty, there is no difference in the incidence between men and women. Alzheimer's disease is the ninth most important factor leading to death over age sixty-five. To date, some research suggests that an active, stimulated mind and a planned exercise program can deter the disease. Additional therapy for women also includes estrogen replacement, anti-inflammatory agents, and antioxidants—but so far none have been definitively proven to work.

SEX AND SEXUALITY: WHEN FOREVER MEANS FOREVER

Throughout our research for *Retirement Rx,* a good friend has provided us with valuable insights. One time, he advised that if we were serious about getting and keeping our male readers' attention, we should begin the first sentence of each new topic with "Sex . . . !"

There's a lot of good news about sex these days. Research shows that no matter how old you live to be, closeness counts—holding hands, hugging, kissing, words of endearment, good conversations, a flirtatious glance, and of course a good romp with someone you care about all contribute to good mental health. Feeling loved, feeling valued, and feeling sexy are positive attributes that we seek from early adulthood right on through our final winks. Thirty percent of American women between the ages of eighty and one hundred and two are still having sex. And it's 63 percent for men in that same age group. So, Baby Boomers, you *do* have something to look forward to! We are pleased to report that sex at sixty and long after, for both men and women, is alive and well.

These days, corporate America is aiming its advertising directly at us "senior citizens." Medications such as Viagra and Cialis have created a major niche in the prescription drug market, targeted mainly at a male audience—women, too, but mainly men. We can't avoid viewing the huge advertising dollars spent on television ads promising romance and intimacy, since they're placed right on target, where most of us can't miss them—all of our favorite sports programs. The manufacturers of these products have done their homework; the couple we watch is "of a certain age," good-looking but not too good-looking. We could be them. They are active, alive, all smiles, and looking forward to spending some intimate time together. Isn't it refreshing to know that sex and all the intimacy and vigor we radiate because of it aren't over until we are? For the 25 percent of men in our survey who experience erectile dysfunction, these drugs are truly wonderful!

So now we all know it—mature men and women think about, desire, and want to have sex. Here's more happy news from the AARP:

■ Sexual activity seems to have a protective effect on men's health. In the Caerphilly Cohort Study conducted in South Wales, United Kingdom, over a ten-year period, researchers Smith, Frankel, and Yarnell found a 50 percent lower death rate if the men had frequent orgasms (at least twice a week).

■ Men who had frequent orgasms cut down on the incidence of prostate cancer, according to a study reported by another group of researchers.

■ An AARP survey of women and sexuality found that:

■ 49 percent were satisfied with their sex life.

■ 60 percent agree or strongly agree that sexual activity is a critical part of a good relationship.

■ 84 percent disagree or strongly disagree that sex is only for younger people.

Man's desire for sex continues from the day he's born until three days after he dies! (And this goes for plenty of women too!)

However, there are a few more physical challenges—the reality is that testosterone and estrogen levels decrease as we age, and we're not as agile or energized as we were. These are facts of life. They all contribute to a more mature lovemaking, but they don't eliminate the urge for enjoying a sexual relationship.

If you are involved in a new relationship, recognize that sexually transmitted diseases, such as HIV, AIDS, gonorrhea, and syphilis, are still alive, active, and contractible, no matter what your age. Make sure that you and a new partner both agree to a Sexually Transmitted Disease (STD) test before you become sexually committed. According to the federal Centers for Disease Control and Prevention, one in four new diagnoses of HIV-AIDs between 2000 and 2003 was in the 45 and older age group. Know whom you go to bed with and remember that you are having sex with all the previous contacts of your sexual partner. Venereal disease has a long trail. Not the most romantic or passionate of thoughts but certainly the safest. First and foremost, be passionate about getting tested, and then get on with the fun.

Next, remember, whatever his age, a man's sperm is capable of impregnating a woman in her childbearing years. Those sperm may become more sluggish as the male ages but they're still able to make a baby.

THE DIAGNOSIS

We don't think we need to give you a quiz to find out if you are healthy or not—if you smoke, have more than one drink every day, and are sedentary, you've got work to do. Quit smoking, cut back on or eliminate liquor, start eating whole, fresh foods, and start an exercise program. If you are already paying attention to your health, congratulations. Keep focused on maintaining your healthy habits, and find new ones to add. Our prescription can act as an action plan to improve your health, no matter where you fall on the spectrum—from robust to at risk.

THE RETIREMENT DOCS' PRESCRIPTION

Small steps make a big difference over time. We cannot offer a game plan for recognizing illness or depression—those are highly individual issues that need the personal attention of a physician. We will make the assumption that you are visiting your doctor regularly and that both of you are keeping an eye on your overall health and addressing any health issues you are facing. In fact, before embarking on any of the suggestions below, check with your doctor. He or she will be absolutely thrilled that you're making an effort to exercise more, eat better, and keep your mind active!

If you ask me what the ten most important traits for a successful retirement are, I would say the first nine would be a healthy lifestyle.

—RETIREMENT DOCS' SURVEY

■ **Develop a weekly exercise game plan:**

What days can you definitely exercise?

_____

_____

_____

What times of day can you definitely exercise?

_____

_____

_____

What kinds of exercise can you do?

_____

_____

_____

Who among your friends can you enlist to join you?

_____

_____

_____

■ **Keep a food journal:** Use one of several free online food diary Web sites or create your own in a blank book. Even if you think you are a healthy eater, writing down what you consume each day makes you aware of how much you are putting in your mouth. You can also see, after just a week of record keeping, what times of day you "fall apart" and succumb to snacks or fattening foods (for many people it's midmorning and midafternoon). After a week or two, ask yourself:

■ Which foods should I cut out? (French fries, steak)
■ Which foods should I add? (More veggies, whole grains)
■ What are my "fall-apart" foods and when do I eat them? (A bag of chips at 3:00 P.M.)
■ What can I replace my "fall-apart" foods with? List five distraction activities (cleaning out a closet, surfing the Internet, reading, calling a friend . . .) and then list five foods that are more healthful alternatives than, say, potato chips, a bag of salt-free pretzels or vegetable chips (instead of a cookie, some dried fruit).

1. _____
2. _____
3. _____
4. _____
5. _____

1. _____
2. _____
3. _____
4. _____
5. _____

■ **Train Your Brain:** It doesn't matter if you are working full-time or part-time or are completely retired—you have to exercise your brain in ways that are different and distinct from what you do at your job each day. Agility comes from a variety of tasks, and that's true both of physical movement and mental exercise. We urge you to plan three to five activities you can do to challenge your intellect and keep your memory sharp. For example, if you are an accountant, we recommend that you incorporate reading novels and poetry into your weekly routine. Bridge or a good game of poker provides a counterbalance for someone who is engaged in creative activities.

1. _____

2. _____

3. _____

4. _____

5. _____

Without good health, the world can be a narrow and inhospitable place for a retired person. A foundation of healthful practices like the ones we have discussed here will lay the groundwork for long-term vitality. Don't put off working on your well-being. Start today. Start now.

9

TRAIT SEVEN: PASSION AND PURPOSE

Nothing is more dishonorable than an old man, heavy with years, who has no other evidence of having lived long except his age.

—SENECA, ROMAN PHILOSOPHER

The data from our Retirement Docs' Survey made it very clear that passion and purpose are fully intertwined and are crucial to a successful and meaningful retirement. In fact, we found that our highly successful retirees differed from our not-yet-so-highly successful retirees primarily in two key areas. The first was that *all* of our highly successful retirees had a driving passion to stay as physically fit as possible and saw it as an ongoing commitment. To delay and offset changes occurring in restricted retirement's phase four, it's so important that you develop long-lasting passions with purpose in phases one, two, and three, which are mentally *and* physically stimulating. Medical science has proven that keeping both an active mind and an active body will decrease and delay many of later life's disabilities.

The personal mosaic makes you the individual you are . . . reflects the sum total of your habits, your outlook on life, your frame of mind, your spiritual or religious beliefs, and the love you have for those around you.

—ISADORE ROSENFELD, M.D., FROM *LIVE NOW, AGE LATER*

The second area in which the passions of our highly successful retirees differed is that they felt a strong desire to give something back to society and be an active participant in making the world a better place. They devote a lot of their time to the causes they believe in—feeling strongly that the satisfaction they receive from the work outweighs any time commitment. Having a passion for some type of volunteer work cannot be underestimated; it bolsters your identity and has incredibly positive effects for your mental health.

> We were put here on this earth for one purpose and that is to make it a better place. We should, therefore, be contributing members of society. And if the earth, as a result of our having been on it, is a better place than it was before we came, then we have achieved our destiny.
>
> —GEN. JIMMY DOOLITTLE, WORLD WAR II THREE-STAR GENERAL

By *passion* we mean "intense, driving, or overmastering feeling or conviction," and by *purpose* we mean something "set up as an object or end to be attained." (Both of these definitions are from *Merriam-Webster's Collegiate Dictionary*, eleventh edition). These activities are different from leisure pursuits in terms of power, principle, and function. While leisure activities help us to get out of ourselves by entertaining us and allowing us to relax and unwind, passions with purpose involve intense emotion, which sparks compelling action, an energetic and unflagging activity that manifests a person's devotion to a cause or a goal.

Ideal passions are those that engage the body, the brain, and the soul. And the goal shouldn't be easily attainable—involving and engaging us instead in a long-term quest. The process of striving offers the greatest amount of challenge, interest, happiness, and feelings of success. Following a passion can involve stress—but it's a good stress. The best kinds of passions occur when a person's body or mind is stretched to its limits in a voluntary effort to accomplish something difficult and worthwhile. We just read an article about a skilled crossword puzzle whiz, a woman who became renowned in her social circle for her keen ability. Her ongoing passion for puzzles led her to push herself beyond her comfort zone and across the country to the American Crossword Puzzle Tournament. It wasn't about the outcome but rather about her passion to go after new experiences and achieve new heights. It's a great example.

As Mihaly Csikszentmihalyi says in his book *Flow: The Psychology of Optimal Experience* (an excellent book about pursuing passion as the key to happiness):

> *The best moments usually occur when a person's body or mind is stretched to its limits in a voluntary effort to accomplish something that is difficult and worthwhile. Optimal experience is something we* make *happen. . . . Such experiences are not necessarily pleasant at the time they occur. The swimmer's muscles might have ached during his most memorable race, his lungs might have felt like exploding, and he might be dizzy with fatigue—yet these could have been the best moments of his life. . . . In the long run, optimal experiences add up to a sense of mastery—or perhaps better, a sense of* participation *in determining the content of life—that comes as close to what is usually meant by happiness as anything else we can conceivably imagine.*

Csikszentmihalyi's description is also a good explanation of why it is impossible, and probably not even advisable, to continually pursue a passion seven days a week, twelve hours a day. Successful retirees, and people in general, need an active balance of both leisure and passion in their lives. The swimmer in the preceding example surely blows off steam by doing something fun but not particularly challenging after a major accomplishment.

> *My major passion was making a living. Now, in retirement, it is about making a life. I retired from work, not life.*
>
> —Retirement Docs' Survey

Most of us find life before retiring full of purposes and passions which revolve around marriage, family, building that first career, striving for a certain standard of living, educating our children, and working toward fiscal security. It's a good and busy fast track, but then what? What about the purposes and passions we'll need during our long-lived second careers, when great numbers of us will be around for a great many more years?

> *Having reached your goals, you will certainly miss one thing: the process of getting there.*
>
> —MARIE VON EBNER-ESCHENBAC

The best passions are those that evolve over time as we change. Make some selections with a specific goal of seeing you through the physical, mental, and social changes that aging brings with it. For example, let's say you've always been a jazz fan, a passion that is flexible enough to be enjoyed in many different ways through time. You studied the clarinet in high school, college, and after college; you played in a jazz quartet and even had some paying gigs. Your group disbanded owing to time constraints and the need for all of you to get "straight" jobs. You kept playing on the side and practicing, which kept your lungs in good shape. And you continued to listen to the pros play jazz both in live performances and on recordings. You enjoy discussing jazz with other like-minded people of all ages who share your passion, and you joined an Internet e-mail news group devoted to jazz. After retiring, you formed a band with some friends who also love to play—and got a regular gig at the little Italian restaurant downtown. You even convinced a pro to join you on trumpet once in a while. But then, as you grew even older and became disabled, you just didn't have the wind it took to play the clarinet. It was difficult to attend live jazz performances, but you still listened to jazz and you continued to share your knowledge through a lifetime of memories with your Internet news group.

Eva Zeisel, a ceramist and product designer born in 1906, has been making and designing beautiful utilitarian items for decades. She has said in many interviews and in her own book, *Eva Zeisel on Design,* which she wrote and published in 2004, that the only thing she could absolutely rely on in life was her design work and the goal of doing good and making a contribution to society. She has never stopped working, although for many years she has worked with young assistants who, because of her failing eyesight and inability to work clay and other materials with her own hands, carry out her ideas with their eyes and their hands. Her love of design and her passion to create have never been daunted by age, disability, or physical degeneration. As long as her spirit is willing, she finds a way to bring ideas to fruition.

It's great to have an interest that carries on throughout a lifetime, but it's just as important and never too late to pick up new ones:

I knew long before I retired that it was vital for me to have a number of interests, hobbies, and goals and to have them in place before I stepped down. Call it fear of the unknown or call it change; whatever it is, I know myself pretty well, so when I did retire, I immediately filled my newly found free time enjoying my projects. My advice is, don't retire and then look for something; retire while you still have your health, not when it's becoming a problem. To be on the safe side, I have some "just in case" passions I chose solely because they wouldn't require leaving my home.

—RETIREMENT DOCS' SURVEY

I never gave any thought about passions until writing this book. I worked backward to get to know my passions by first figuring out my life's themes and goals for my second career. My first goal was finding substitutes for the "highs" I got from practicing medicine; others were a spinoff from my first career. My passions, which I have taped over my desk at home, are

1. *Doing everything I can to keep my mate happy. This includes taking on some of the housework and expanding specific activities to do with her.*

2. *Being there for my family and our children's families both emotionally and fiscally. We are lucky because we were able, with expert financial advice, to set up trust funds for our grandchildren's college educations. It makes us feel like we can leave them with education, a part of us that we really care a lot about—and that makes us feel great.*

3. *Having a structured plan to work on the eight traits outlined in this book, especially a healthy lifestyle.*

4. *Doing multiple activities that are productive and related particularly to medicine; ongoing research, writing, updating previously published textbooks, and staying mentally challenged as long as possible.*

5. *Developing a passion for helping myself and other people have a successful second career.*

—DR. FRITZ

Because Retirement Rx *was not available for me, as the years passed by, I did the things that seemed to be the right thing to do at the time. I think I did a pretty good job of selecting a wide range of passions and purposes that interested me at various stages of my life; I just didn't give them labels. There was no science to it, just a "feeling" of what I wanted to do. Many opportunities were offered— I accepted some and rejected others. My first marriage ended in divorce after twenty years, but those years produced three wonderful children. My second marriage is still going strong after twenty-five years—creating a blended family and offering me more understanding of all that life has to offer. My conclusion is that passion and purpose never stop, and that realization has made me a very happy man.*

—DR. JIM

Many of us find purpose with passion at home with our family. Having time to engage with them after retirement allows us to become active participants in our children's, grandchildren's, and great-grandchildren's development. Others of us find passion in caregiving as we age—taking care of loved ones out of necessity and love can be deeply meaningful and satisfying for many people. But the added responsibilities of looking after another person as we age are accompanied by emotional and physical challenges. Finding and chasing your passion and purpose is about balance. It's important to find and follow passions that excite you, but take time for self-care if that passion involves looking after others.

As one of our respondents noted:

It dawned on me one day that many of my friends had become caregivers, giving their time and talents to their incapacitated mates. And every so often, those friends passed away before their loved ones. I think that administering this loving care as a primary purpose cheated my friends out of some of their prime time.

—RETIREMENT DOCS' SURVEY

DIAGNOSIS

If you want to make sure that you don't feel aimless after you stop working, serious contemplation is required before you retire. If you are a retiree, take a look at the rest of your life and how you want to spend it. Realize that it's never, ever, too late to answer the following questions and apply them to how you want to see yourself. Take time to write down the answers and revisit them from time to time. A retirement that can last thirty or forty years of pointlessly filling time not only leads to depression but is a missed opportunity to leave something behind—a legacy of wisdom, or charity, or actual physical creation. Your legacy need not receive notoriety beyond your own family to have deep and lasting meaning or impact. Those who remember your contributions will doubtless carry them on into the rest of their lives in one way or another.

- Have you thought about *what* you want to achieve in retirement?

  _____
  _____
  _____

- Do you have purposeful goals for your second career?

  _____
  _____
  _____

- Have you thought about *who* you want to be and how you would best like to be remembered?

  _____
  _____
  _____

■ Do you know *how* you're going to accomplish your objectives?

_____

_____

■ How many things do you currently feel passionate about? Can you identify the purposes behind your passions?

_____

_____

■ What are the activities you do that you find completely absorbing? What things do you do that you get lost in—the kind of things that seem as if you've spent only a couple of hours at and it turns out that you're wondering where the day went?

_____

_____

■ Are your purposes easily attainable? Does it surprise you that they shouldn't be? You can't be passionate without an ongoing goal.

_____

_____

■ Can you list five, ten, or more purposeful undertakings that will serve you well from the present right on through your final farewell?

_____

_____

■ Do you have passions that make you available to people, as well as societal and environmental needs? Do you give more of yourself than you want in return?

_____

_____

_____

■ Do you have passions that will continue to promote a healthy lifestyle?

_____

_____

_____

■ Are you thinking ahead to second-career passions that will weather the storms of possible and probable age-related limitations or medical setbacks? Can you list them?

_____

_____

_____

I am lucky enough to have a ninety-four-year-old, bright and active grandmother who has a true passion for living. She told me that before she gets out of bed each morning, she makes a plan, or I guess it's more a question and an answer, anyway her kind of plan. She figures out what she can do that day to make someone else's life a little bit easier. She may send a note or card to a grandchild or do something for a neighbor like visiting or baking banana bread. These seem like small things, but their effect is great. The passion to show love to others could be the greatest purpose of all. That is what she does everyday. My grandmother remains a joy and an inspiration to our entire family.

—RETIREMENT DOCS' SURVEY

THE RETIREMENT DOCS' PRESCRIPTION

Take the answers from the previous set of questions and use them to identify the person you want to be, along with the goals you hope to accomplish and how you'll go about *being* and *doing* them. Then, make a list of pursuits that are engaging enough to become deeply involved in. This is not the same as making a commitment to taking care of your health or exercising on a regular basis. Those are activities we would classify as "maintenance behaviors." It's also not the same as leisure stuff you do for fun and relaxation. List the loves, interests, causes, ideas, and hobbies that you can lose yourself in. Make a note of when you can begin to act on each. Can you start right away (there's no time like the present)? Or is it something that requires more time, and you will begin it when you are fully retired? Knowing when you can start something makes planning for it easier, and the anticipation is more pleasurable.

Take a look at these specific suggestions gathered from highly successful retirees. They just might help you get on with or add to your own retirement.

- Learning about fresh, local, and seasonal ingredients from my local farmer's market. This is both in an effort to expand my culinary abilities and a way of getting to know local growers, and to become involved in the sustainability movement, which is important to me. Cooking with fresh whole foods also contributes to a healthy lifestyle.
- Learning to fish for "big game" in the ocean. Fly-fishing is fun, but I want to master offshore fishing and see if I can bag a marlin or tuna. I want to compete in tournaments. It's a sport that requires strength, concentration, and dexterity. It's also good exercise. And it's going to give me a chance to pursue another passion—travel. The best big-game fishing happens to take place in all the places I want to go but have never seen, like the coast of California, the eastern coastline of Australia, Hawaii, and South America.
- Volunteering my marketing and writing skills in the next presidential election. I want to work at a grassroots level and pass on my knowledge to young staffers. And I want to get my candidate elected!
- Start a skateboard business. I love sports and young people. Skateboarding is making a comeback. It's a good business to be in right now. I love the designs on skateboards, and I am actually designing my own board in my workshop, which I plan to sell in my shop. And I'm still young enough to do a few turns myself.
- Run for office. I am going to throw my hat in the mayoral ring in my town.

■ I have been reading mysteries for more than forty years and consider myself an expert at every murder technique, twist, and surprise ending. So now I am going to write one—actually I am going to write a series. I have a "continuing" character in mind and a setting. I have the first plot planned out. I may even have a first draft done before I retire completely.

■ I never finished college, so I am enrolling. My plan is to get a degree in art history. I have been volunteering at the local children's museum for several years, helping them plan fund-raisers and charity events. They have recently asked me to sit on their board of trustees. I feel it's my obligation to complete my studies so I can make a greater contribution to the institution.

■ Hike the entire Appalachian Trail before I can't walk anymore! I'm starting next month.

■ See Europe. I might even stay a while. I've always wanted to live in France. I might even be able to get a job there, since I understand that there is a labor shortage all over Western Europe.

■ There are a few things I'm interested in that center on wellness— hospice work, yoga, and meditation. I am already working toward yoga certification, and hope to teach classes and bring my knowledge to hospices, where I think it can do a lot of good.

■ Collect every Louis Armstrong recording ever made. I have amassed a pretty impressive collection, but there are still several sides I'm missing. I search on eBay, have joined 78-record auction lists, and scour record bins in antique stores wherever I am (they are usually in cardboard boxes under tables). Then I plan to catalog my finds, and compile them on my fourteen-year-old grandson's iPod (with his help). Hurrah for him, hurrah for me—he's showing an interest in the trumpet.

I feel it is very important to have a purpose in retirement like I had during my working years, a reason to get up in the morning.

—RETIREMENT DOCS' SURVEY

We hope you embrace finding your passions as a chance to learn about the subjects that have always intrigued you but that you never had time to pursue—an opportunity to explore the world in-depth, the luxury of time on your side working *for* you, not against you. What a chance we have to live optimally, enthusiastically, and with the wonder and curiosity of a child, but with the advantage of wisdom. Enjoy.

10

TRAIT EIGHT: LET THE SPIRIT MOVE YOU— SPIRITUALITY AND RELIGION

The human quest for spiritual understanding passes through multiple lenses of experience. To some it comes in Scripture; others find the message etched in nature. To some it is unfolded in endless variety. To some it is fostered by rule; to others it is being free. The spiritual quest, whatever the course, has elevated the human spirit. It has tapped genius, created music, inspired poetry, nurtured ethical systems, and become philosophy. Deep within each person is a spiritual longing. It is a thirst unquenched, a hunger unfulfilled, a vision only partly seen.

—RALPH WALDO EMERSON

Highly successful retirees specifically pinpoint spirituality/religion as necessary for retirement success. In life's final chapter, we will all look back over a lifetime of what we did or what we didn't do and what we might have done differently. We said it before: as doctors we know when to refer out. We're a good team for ongoing dialogue. Dr. Fritz is searching for what spirituality means in his quest for a guaranteed retirement, and Dr. Jim is a cradle Catholic. Boy, have we had some great discussions!

What is spirituality? Dictionaries define it as relating to or having the nature of spirit; a state of being concerned with affecting the soul, which is neither tangible nor material. We've heard others describe it simply as anything outside yourself that gives you comfort or solace. The conventional expression of it is organized religion. However, as Ralph Waldo Emerson points out in the epigram that opens this chapter, spirituality can take many other forms.

Where two or more gather together in recognition of a power greater than themselves, to listen to the inner life—where music lives.

—GEORGE E. VALLIANT, AUTHOR

According to two gerontology scholars, Nancy Hooyman and H. Asuman Kiyak, "Spirituality or spiritual well-being can be differentiated from organized religion and is defined as the following:

■ Self-determined wisdom in which the individual tries to achieve stability in his or her environment.
■ Self-transcendence or crossing a boundary beyond the self in which the individual adjusts to loss and rejects material security.
■ Achievement of meaning and purpose for one's continued existence.
■ Acceptance of the wholeness of life."

We questioned priests, preachers, and rabbis, listened to the Dalai Lama, interviewed agnostics and atheists, and talked with a range of people whose beliefs and spiritual needs are met through the sun, the moon, the earth, and the galaxies. We have even taken meditation classes. And we've concluded that until our lives are over, we can't give you any definitive answers about spirituality, and we certainly cannot tell you what religion or belief system is best for you in retirement. The one constant is that the afterlife is a mystery, and it's up to each of us to decide how to make sense of it. What we *can* do is share what we've learned about how spirituality specifically relates to retirement.

Sometimes, when I think about my life and my faith, I revert to childhood memories and how life does indeed come full circle. When I was a little girl, my teddy

bear meant the world to me. There was nothing make-believe about the compan-
ionship, support, and security he provided. When my son was just a little guy, his
blanket gave him the same stability. And most of my grandchildren had a similar
need for sharing with a pretend friend. It occurred to me one day that now that I
am older and my religion offers me such comfort and safety, I really have done
nothing more than find my "grown-up" support. My life really has come full circle.

—Retirement Docs' Survey

Our Retirement Docs' Survey asked respondents to rate the importance of spirituality/religion in their lives by checking one of the following: extremely important, very important, important, somewhat important, or not very important. We then correlated and separately compared each of retirement's four phases against every respondent's answer. In the first three phases of our participants' retirements, there was no statistical difference in one group over the other regarding their responses to the faith question. In fact, it was the least important of the eight traits. It became clear that spirituality/religion religion tends to change only late in life.

We found that in phase four there was a statistically significant jump in faith-based involvement when we compared our top 20 percent against the rest of the group. When we analyzed our data, it was apparent that we had our hands on information that we had not seen reported before: In order to have a highly successful retirement you've got to have some form of spirituality in phase four. Some form of spirituality became a must-have trait for our highly successful retirees in the final stage of their retirements (and their lives).

Our top 20 percent reported that their faith provided them with a sense of inspiration and a source of hope outside of themselves, a happier, healthier lifestyle, a needed calm and inner strength, support for the normal process of aging, and for help in coping with chronic illness, death of loved ones, isolation, and overall depression. Approaching our life's final years, major adjustments, both physical and mental, will occur. Each and every one of us will see a shift in our priorities—all we know is that being born is fatal. Facing restricted retirement without the support spirituality provides can be an enormous challenge.

Have Faith in the Facts

According to a recent Gallup Poll:

- 96 percent of Americans believe in God or a universal spirit.
- 90 percent pray.
- 85 percent say spirituality or religion is very or fairly important to them.
- 41 percent attend religious services weekly.
- 48 percent of eighteen- to twenty-nine-year-olds say religion is very important to them.
- 73 percent of Americans older than age sixty-five say the same.

If you're feeling shaky at this point, reflecting back over your past history of sitting through sermons that seemed as if they would never end and going through the motions of a religion that may have turned you off to God when you were younger, relax. Psychologists and researchers have found that the positive effects of spirituality on mental health are not limited to participation in organized religions. Clinical studies have found that the benefits of a strong faith, in whatever form it takes, include improved self-esteem, a stronger immune system, lower blood pressure, better social skills, a greater will to live, a decrease in stress, and a positive image of aging. Many Boomers are searching for or using a more practical and individualistic rather than doctrinal approach. Eastern philosophies, Jungian psychology, self-help groups, and a long list of other alternatives are emerging among Boomers, who for whatever reason have turned away from their childhood religions, or are taking bits and pieces from each religion to form an individual spiritual philosophy.

When my husband died, I replaced his role in my life with spirituality. I continue to take daily walks, talking my problems over with the universe . . . this may or may not necessarily be God. Often it seems like it's just nature—the trees, the flowers, or the birds. But in my walks, I'm talking to somebody or something greater than myself. I kind of turn things over to an "extra spirit." By the time I get back home, I always feel better.

—RETIREMENT DOCS' SURVEY

MAYBE YOU SHOULD GET ORGANIZED

Organized religion enters many people's lives in some way around puberty, levels off, then becomes stronger in our late twenties or early thirties, coinciding with the time most of us start a family. During midlife, religion remains level unless adversity occurs. In our survey, there's another spike in religious involvement one more time in later life (phase four). And while we said earlier that it is not necessary to attend formal religious services on a weekly basis to get the health benefits of faith, there is a clear preference for organized religion among seniors (people over sixty-five).

More seniors belong to Christian churches or Jewish synagogues than all other community nonreligious organizations combined. This high percentage of believers indicates that formalized religion fills a human need for more of us than does any other spiritual expression or a lack of a faith. For many, belonging to an organized group offers the opportunity to find support among those who share a common set of traditions, beliefs, values, and practices. It also expresses a common way of life through liturgies, stories, and disciplines.

The pastor of a large congregation told us that he feels that the increase in the number of elderly women joining his church, compared to men of the same age (outside of mortality or disability rates), is because women spend more time thinking about the past. They have by nature a more spiritual conscience, and religion offers them an understanding of their lives as well as comfort. He felt that men more often reviewed their lives in much broader terms: "Did I lead a good life? Did I do more good than harm? Did I lead an honest life?" Affirmative answers to those questions offer comfort when facing adversity, and many senior males can outline their faith and their personal spirituality through them.

Lifelong religious conviction remained strong throughout retirement for people who had parochial school educations and for those who attended religious services on a regular basis during their working years. But it was often the people who lived with excess trauma, especially if they were able to successfully deal with their setbacks, who had the strongest faith later in their lives. Religious beliefs can become a formalized coping mechanism for these individuals.

Raised awareness of the inevitability of death and a search for life's meaning may well act as an important catalyst propelling adults toward thoughts about the end of life. It is a telling fact that for assistance with personal problems, more senior "believers" sought advice from their clergy than from their doctors. It's a time of self-reflection and self-analysis, looking back on life's accomplishments, disappointments, and transgressions. And it's a period when many unsolvable traumas occur, often with minimal time in between for recovery. We find ourselves wanting something or someone to believe in beyond ourselves, a system providing solace and comfort.

During my first ten years of marriage I think I unknowingly (or I choose to tell myself it was unknowingly) convinced myself that my wife and children were number one in my life when number one was really establishing my career. My wife told both herself and me that I was number one, whereas number one was really raising the family. Now in my later years, number one is honestly about us and looking together for answers to what our purpose is here on Earth. I guess it's a different kind of achieving at a different time of life.

—RETIREMENT DOCS' SURVEY

Yet another key role in organized religion is its ability to be responsive to the social needs of senior citizens. Up to a third of the senior population is severely depressed at some time during phase four's restricted retirement. Depression occurs in people with and without religious beliefs, but the support of a formal religious practice has multiple benefits. Religious seniors have less depression, fewer suicides, better subjective well-being, more satisfaction with life, and higher self-esteem.

> *Retirement has given me the opportunity to be more active in volunteering in my church and civic organizations. Reaching out to others, sharing ideas, meeting others with like ideas. My motto: Don't lose who you are and what you like to do. Be active and involved, and keep making friends.*
>
> —RETIREMENT DOCS' SURVEY

One of the people we turned to for research and insight as we were working on this chapter is a good friend, Father Howard Lincoln. A man of unquestioning faith, he is a real Catholic go-getter and gatherer of the followers. His parish is located in Palm Desert, California, and throughout the week he draws several thousand to hear what he's got to say. When we sent him a rough chapter outline, he recognized in one of our respondent's comments, copied below, the philosopher Blaise Pascal's idea that we might as well choose to believe that God exists because it might lead to eternal life and happiness; and if it turns out He doesn't exist, nothing would be lost. If we don't believe and we are wrong, we could be in trouble:

> *Someone once asked me if I believed in God. I've heard the answer I gave a few times before and it still makes perfect sense to me. You bet I do. Since I don't know what's waiting for me on the other side, why not have some faith? I have nothing to lose. If there is a God, I'm on the winning team, and if there isn't, well, my religion has offered me some great guidelines.*
>
> —RETIREMENT DOCS' SURVEY

Whatever else our survey respondent had in common with Pascal, we *do* know that the two of them thought alike on at least one thing—you might as well hedge your bets and start believing in something. The benefits of doing so in the here and now are tangible and quantifiable, and as far as the hereafter goes. . . .

DIAGNOSIS

So, how do you know if you are spiritual or religious?

Is there a measuring stick? If you find one, please contact us and share it. Each of us makes this determination based on our philosophy, our own coping skills, adaptive skills, and stress-reducing mechanisms that we find outside ourselves. It's normal if your assessments fluctuate from month to month or even day to day.

THE RETIREMENT DOCS' PRESCRIPTION

I know the God who created me and because I do, I find it easier to be content with what I have and those I live with. I let God be in charge of my life and I'm not afraid to try anything. God will correct my progress if it needs correcting.

—RETIREMENT DOCS' SURVEY

Religious or spiritual growth arises for a wide range of practical reasons. Again, as medical doctors, we can't help you develop or find the type of spirituality the suits you, but we can review with you various prescriptions that have provided other people comfort.

If it hasn't been a part of your life before entering your second career, this spiritual trait is one of the most, if not *the* most, difficult to achieve. Unfortunately, if you didn't have a strong religious background during your childhood or in your first career, religion is often difficult to realize in your second. Some of the best prescriptions for finding and using religion that we can provide come from comments on our Retirement Docs' Survey from respondents. To the point and briefly, they told us how they felt about their lives and their spirituality. For example, one person succinctly described religion and aging with elegant perspective when he wrote, "Religious beliefs and common sense allow me to age gracefully, accepting inevitability. Katharine Hepburn told it like it was when she said, 'Growing old ain't for sissies.' I put my relationship with God first in all my plans. He directs me to what and where I am. Generally speaking, old age is not easy or comfortable, but with God leading the way, I know an inner peace."

Others felt that early morning spiritual reading, joining a community of fellow seekers, and regular prayer from the heart all helped them move closer to the source of spiritual inspiration in their lives. When nurtured, the source slowly strengthened over time and gave them a newfound sense of inner power. Still others felt that attending church provided them with a passion in life, and something meaningful to replace the hours they had spent at a job. "My church activities have provided that resource," one wrote.

Another said spirituality helped ease the stress of illness: "Needing to find joy in my life while living with illness proved a challenge. I was drawn to people and sought a compassionate community in which to share my struggles and gain spiritual support. The gifts of courage, trust, and wisdom came to me through people sharing their stories." One respondent told us that she used religion to clean out her soul. "I worked on getting rid of pettiness, forgiving myself and others, and clearing out negative baggage that I've been dragging around way too long. This spiritual release allows me to let go of my stress and makes more room for love. I'm far from success, but I keep at it."

> *I am highly spiritual: I have faith in my family, I have faith in nature, and I have faith in science.*
>
> —RETIREMENT DOCS' INTERVIEW

There is no standard, FDA-approved prescription for achieving your own spirituality. This is your own personal quest. The sooner it is in place and established, the greater chance for your success in protecting yourself later in life.

■ The essence of most religions are love, forgiveness, and the belief in and acceptance of God. This for most of us should be the backbone of spirituality. To the end, make peace with your family and friends. Use your love to give back to society. And, for the religious, try to find a meaningful place in your heart for God.

- There are no do-overs in life. Learn to accept the life that was handed you and the way you played the cards. Accept disappointments and move on. Do not dwell on your past mistakes—no one is perfect—learn to love and forgive yourself.

- Emphasize the good deeds or things (or whatever you want to call them) you have done in your life; take stock of them consciously and purposefully—it will give you comfort and inner peace as one ages. We should all have an instant-recall memory bank full of warm fuzzies—those acts of kindness or grace we bestowed on others and those that were directed by others to us. These fond memories can help warm up an otherwise bleak day.

- Take up a spiritual quest by reading, questioning, meditating, and exploring religion and various forms of spirituality.

- Review your life—hunt for that "spark" that gave your life meaning and expand on it. At various phases of life, there are transitory "sparks" that last a lifetime and affect your inner being/soul.

- Take on the role of "wise elder" in your family, keeper of family traditions, historian and counselor. This can be expanded to a similar role as advisor or consultant in volunteer efforts, community affairs, or group activities.

- Embrace your spirituality/religion so that it becomes more center-stage later in life, as material things become less so.

- For some, the form of spirituality that comes to you may not be as important as something outside yourself that gives you comfort and solace.

- For many at the late stages of life their greatest comfort comes from family, or extended family. Often, this is the "spark" in phases one, two, three, and four.

- Accept the natural process of all living things; birth, growth, maturity, aging, and death. To achieve an inner peace as we approach our own mortality, we are helped by the awareness that we are completing a natural life cycle; death is a normal part of that cycle. Acceptance of this notion is paramount, whether you also rely on religious beliefs of reincarnation or of heaven and hell.

■ Organized religion is the gold standard of spirituality for most. Baby Boomers seem to be leaning toward the philosophy of author Ken Kesey: "Take what you can, and leave the rest go." Some forms of spirituality may stand alone or be additive to religion.

Don't fret if you find it difficult to allow the spirit to move you. Awe of the universe or God comes with time. For now, a line taken from an old African-American spiritual offers good counsel: "I'm doing the best I can with what I've got." Do the best with whatever beliefs you have, and expand on them. If you are currently connected to a religion or spiritual movement, preretirement and retirement are the perfect time to become more deeply involved in it, particularly those activities that put you in contact with other attending members. The more deeply you become involved in your spiritual community now, the better off you will be later on—when the social and spiritual services it offers can provide support when you need it most, in the third and fourth phases of retirement.

PART THREE

■ ■ ■

THE EXIT CONSULTATION

Some wise person once said: *"Beautiful young people are creations of nature; beautiful old people create themselves."*

—Anonymous

To which we add: *"Beautiful people in their retirement create themselves from the inside out."*

—Retirement Docs' Survey

As we said at the beginning of our journey, retirement offers you the opportunity to create your life as you want it to be, to define it as you wish, and to live it the way you want to. Don't miss out on this incredible opportunity. This is the essence of *Retirement Rx.* And just as we do when a patient is about to leave the doctor's office, we're going to briefly recap what we've done, and send you out with a few final words of advice about your future highly successful retirement.

11

INTO THE FUTURE

Age only matters when one is aging. Now that I have reached a great age, I might as well be twenty.

—PABLO PICASSO

In the data we obtained from our Retirement Docs' Survey, the top 20 percent of our respondents, known as the highly successful retirees, taught us that if we paid attention to what they had to teach us, then practiced what they had to teach us, and then perfected what they had to teach us, we could be as they were—guaranteed highly successful retirements. Our information was groundbreaking, authentic, scientific data, and we found it awe-inspiring. From that information we were able to identify eight traits that made up the backbone of the guarantee, which are described in detail in the previous pages.

Each trait must be operational in order for you to achieve a highly successful retirement, though some of the traits serve more important roles at different times in the four phases. It's an absolute given that the eight traits are never stagnant but are evolving and interdependent in multifaceted ways. Weaving back and forth and into one another, they circle in and out at phase boundaries, as well as ebbing and flowing like tidal currents throughout our second careers. The traits necessary for a highly successful retirement are so interdependent that failure in just one of them can cause dysfunction in multiple areas. Success in a specific trait demands the support of anywhere from two to six of the others. Take, for example, the trait "go with the flow," or "the ability to accept change." In order for it to work, it requires the additional support of several of the traits, including planning, a strong support system, a healthy lifestyle, leisure, a positive attitude, and a good dose of spirituality. If any one of the six required is lacking you will have a tough time accepting change.

Stay vigilant in maintaining the traits. Unfortunately, a trait may be performing well and then, for any number of reasons, can weaken, and your retirement success will be in limbo until the trait is up and working again.

We recommend that you take the Retirement Docs' Quiz whenever you enter a new phase, or when something major in your life happens, to see how you're doing. It's especially important when you're entering a new phase. It's a quick way to identify the traits that might need your attention.

We found that most of our highly successful retirees who had life partners planned for their futures as a team, especially when moving into another phase. When we looked at the data collected from all of our survey respondents and then identified all of those with mates we found the following: in total 37 percent of them worked as a team planning and preparing both fiscal and nonfiscal aspects, 28 percent to a large extent, 15 percent to a moderate extent, 11 percent to some extent, and only 9 percent had very little joint involvement.

Besides taking the Retirement Docs' Quiz periodically, it's a good idea to get together with your mate and write down your short-term goals (one year from retirement); and your long-term goals for the next three to five years. It works best if you make your lists independently and then compare and discuss them. Some guidelines to consider are new leisure activities, employment, family relationships, travel plans, health issues, and how long you see yourselves as being really fit and what you want to achieve in that time. Make it an action plan for accomplishing what works for you.

We have had so many more years of good health than did our parents. We never expected or thought about all the things we could look forward to. My husband and I plan where we want to live, what we want to do, what we want to accomplish, and what we see as our goals and our legacy. It's a great time in our lives.

—RETIREMENT DOCS' SURVEY

Whether you're in phase one, approaching retirement, or fully into phase four, be aware of the great power you possess through the multitude of senior services available to you and yours. Peruse the Retirement Resources on pages 181–183. We've compiled a partial listing, partial because every day introduces new possibilities and a changing list. Look these over and be amazed at what is out there for us. When Goldie Hawn and Paul McCartney are featured in AARP's monthly magazine, we know we're "cutting-edge," baby! We've got the power—let's use it.

Writing this book helped us so much to age with grace, energy, love, and laughter. We've come to look at and accept that aging is a natural part of living. After all, we come into the world doing it, and as far as we know, it's not going to stop until we do.

The *Retirement Rx* exploration has led to a better understanding of ourselves, and it has made us better people, husbands, and fathers. We know the direction that we want our lives to take—and that will happen just as long as we keep working on and developing our own eight traits. We must admit that we're not quite at the guaranteed level yet, close but no gold stars (or should that read gold watches?). We both need more points on the Retirement Docs' Quiz, but by fine-tuning a couple of the traits and working especially on healthy lifestyle for Dr. Jim and spirituality for Dr. Fritz— hey, we're getting closer.

All of us want to make our track record equal a successful life's run. Identifying and adjusting any of the problems retirement can throw across your path and having the ability to choose correct solutions will keep you in the race and way ahead of most of the pack. We hope that *Retirement Rx* gives you the map to make your decision making easier, decrease problems along the way, and make your run a victorious one.

We are, as always, inspired by the ability of Ralph Waldo Emerson to put what we feel into just the right words. We quoted him earlier in the book and he's here again. We hope he was enjoying a highly successful retirement (he lived to be seventy-nine) when he wrote the following:

To laugh often and love much; to win the respect of intelligent persons and the affection of children; to earn the approbation of honest citizens and endure the betrayal of false friends; to appreciate beauty; to find the best in others; to give of one's self; to leave the world a bit better, whether by a healthy child, a garden patch or a redeemed social condition; to have played and laughed with enthusiasm and sung with exultation; to know that even one life has breathed easier because you have lived—this is to have succeeded.

We invite your stories and comments at www.theretirementdocs.com.

CONCLUSION

To know how to grow old is the masterwork of wisdom, and one of the most difficult chapters in the great art of living.

—HENRI-FRÉDÉRIC AMIEL

Here is our favorite collection of wisdom gleaned from Retirement Docs' Survey respondents, the people who have walked the walk. At least 20 percent of them, those highly successful retirees, figured out how to get the most out of their retirement years. We set off their words or tips or suggestions here in the hope that you will photocopy the list and keep it in a place where you will see it—and read through it—every day.

- Make a "to-do" list each day, and cross off everything completed by the end of the day.
- Keep your sense of humor.
- Life is fragile, so live each day to its fullest, and treat it and yourself with respect.
- Enjoy yourself. You can learn to be your own best company.
- Plan for the unexpected along with the expected.
- Retire to something, not from something.
- It's better to have halitosis than no breath at all.

- Challenge your interests. Work part-time or volunteer your talents.
- Nurture friendships. To have a friend, you have to be a friend.
- Plan to live longer than you expect to.
- Compromise is the name of the game. Spousal agreement is the goal!
- Any morning that you can smell the coffee is a great morning.
- Try new things. If they don't suit you, try something else. You won't have any fun if you wait for someone to knock on your door.
- Be prepared for no days off!

SOURCES

CHAPTER ONE: A NEW KIND OF RETIREMENT

AARP. "New AARP study finds Boomers vary in their views of the future and their retirement years." (1998) www.aarp.org/press/1998/nr060298.html

Bolles R.N. *The Three Boxes of Life and How to Get Out of Them.* Berkeley: Ten Speed Press, 1978.

Buford, B. *Stuck in Half-Time: Reinvesting Your One and Only Life.* Grand Rapids: Zondervan Publishing House, 2001.

Cantor, D, and A. Thompson. *What Do You Want to Do When You Grow Up? Starting the Next Chapter of Your Life.* Boston: Little, Brown and Company, 2002.

Diamond, J. "Zebras, Unhappy Marriages, and the Anna Karenina Principle." *Guns, Germs, and Steel: The Fates of Human Societies.* New York: W. W. Norton & Company, 2001.

Freedman, Marc. *Prime Time: How Baby Boomers Will Revolutionize Retirement and Transform America.* NewYork: Public Affairs, 1999.

Fyock, C. D., and A. M. Dorton. *UnRetirement: A Career Guide for the Retired . . . the Soon-to-Be-Retired . . . the Never-Want-to-Be Retired.* New York: American Management Association, 1994.

Kaplan, L. J. *Retirement Right: Planning for Your Successful Retirement.* Garden City Park, New York: Avery Publishing Group Inc., 2003.

Olshansky, S. K., and B. A. Carnes. *The Quest for Immortality: Science at the Frontiers of Aging.* New York: W. W. Norton & Company, 2003.

Sheldon A., P. J. M. McEwan, and C. P. Ryser. *Retirement: Patterns and Predictions.* Rockville, Md.: National Institute of Mental Health, Section on Mental Health of the Aging, 1975.

Walker, J. W., D. C. Kimmel and K. F. Price. "Retirement Style and Retirement Satisfaction: Retirees Aren't All Alike." *International Aging and Human Development* 12(4): 267–80, 1980.

Weiss S. S., and E. H. Kaplan. "Inner Obstacles to Psychoanalysts' Retirement: Personal, Clinical and Theoretical Perspectives." *Bulletin of the Menninger Clinic* 64(4): 443–61, 2000.

CHAPTER TWO: THE RETIREMENT DOCS' QUIZ

CHAPTER THREE: TRAIT ONE: SOWING SEEDS— THE PLANNER'S ADVANTAGE

Bernstein, A., and J. Trauth. *Your Retirement, Your Way: Why it Takes More than Money to Live Your Dream.* Los Angeles: McGraw-Hill, 2006.

Fletcher, D. *Life After Work: Redefining Retirement—A Step-by-Step Guide to Balancing Your Life and Achieving Bliss in the Wisdom Years.* Bangor, Me.: Booklocker.com, 2007.

Helen, M., and S. Smith. *101 Secrets for a Great Retirement.* Los Angeles: McGraw-Hill, 2000.

Hudson, F. M. *The Adult Years: Mastering the Art of Self-Renewal.* San Francisco: Jossey-Bass Publishers, 1999.

Leibowitz, M. *Charting a Course in Rough Financial Seas. TIAA –CREF Participant* (May 2001), pp. 5–10.

Leider, R., and D. Shapiro. *Repacking Your Bags—Lighten Your Load for the Rest of Your Life*, 2nd ed. San Francisco: Berrett-Koehler, 1995.

Mark-Jarvis, Gail. *Saving for Retirement Without Living Like a Pauper or Winning the Lottery.* Upper Saddle River, N.J.: Pearson Education Inc., 2007.

Older American 2000: Key Indicators of Well-being. Federal Interagency Forum on Aging Related Statistics, 2000.

Stewart, L. *So What Are You Doing with Yourself These Days?* PaineWebber, 1993.

CHAPTER FOUR: TRAIT TWO: ACCENTUATE THE POSITIVE—IT'S ALL ABOUT ATTITUDE

Canning, D., and P. Canning. "Retired Life Fun: Retirement—Make It Your Golden Age." www.retiredlifefun.com/rlf3a.htm (accessed 6/27/2000).

Chang, E. C. *Optimism and Pessimism.* Washington D.C.: American Psychological Association, 2001.

Kimmell, D., K. Price, and J. Walker. "Retirement Choice and Retirement Satisfaction." *Journal of Gerontology* 33, no.4 (1978): 575–85.

Newberry, T. *Success Is Not an Accident.* Decatur, Ga.: Looking Glass Books, 2000.

Oskamp, Stewart, and P. Wesley Shultz. *Attitudes and Opinions.* Florence, Ky.: Lawrence Erlbaum, 2004.

Peterson, C., and M.E.P. Seligman. *Character Strengths and Virtues: A Handbook and Classification.* American Psychological Association, Oxford University Press, 2004.

Scheier, M., C. Carver, and M. Bridges. "Distinguishing Optimism from Neuroticism (and Trait Anxiety, Self-Mastery, and Self-Esteem): A Reevaluation of the Life Orientation Test." *Journal of Personality and Social Psychology* 67, no. 6 (1994): 1063–78.

Seligman, M.E.P., *Learned Optimism: How to Change Your Mind and Your Life.* New York: Simon and Schuster, 1998.

Snyder, C. R., and S. J. Lopez. "Optimistic Explanatory Style." *The Handbook of Positive Psychology.* London: Oxford University Press, 2002.

Chapter Five: Trait Three: Go with the Flow— Accept Change

Baruth K. E., and J. J. Carroll. "A Formal Assessment of Resilience: The Baruth Protective Factors Inventory." *Journal of Individual Psychology,* 58, no. 3 (2002): 235–44.

Bergeman, C. S. and K. A. Wallace. "Resiliency in Later Life." *Life-Span Perspectives on Health and Illness.* T. L. Whitman, T. V. Merluzzi, and R. D. White, eds. Mahwah, N.J.: Lawrence Erlbaum, 1999, pp. 207–25.

Bonanno, G. A., J. T. Moskowitz, and A. Papa, et al. "Resilience to Loss in Bereaved Spouses, Bereaved Parents, and Bereaved Gay Men." *Journal of Personality and Social Psychology* 88, no. 5 (2005): 827–53.

Bonanno, G. A. and C. B. Wortman, et al. "Resilience to Loss and Chronic Grief: A Prospective Study from Preloss to 18-months Postloss," *Journal of Personality and Social Psychology* 83, no. 5 (2002): 1150–64.

Brzowsky, Sara. "How to Be Stress-Resilient." *Parade Magazine,* October 12, 2003, pp. 10–12.

Glover, R. J. "Perspectives on Aging: Issues Affecting the Latter Part of the Life Cycle." *Educational Gerontology* 24 (1998): 325–31.

Hooker, K. and D. Ventis. "Work Ethic, Daily Activities, and Retirement Satisfaction." *Journal of Gerontology* 39, no. 4 (1984): 478–84.

Langer, N. "The Importance of Spirituality in Later Life." *Gerontology and Geriatrics Education* 20, no. 3 (2000): 41–50.

Leider, R. J., and D. A. Shapiro. *Repacking Your Bags: Lighten Your Load for the Rest of Your Life,* 2nd ed. San Francisco: Berrett-Koehler, Inc., 1995.

Lopez, S. J., and C. R. Snyder. *Handbook of Positive Psychology.* New York: Oxford University Press, 2002.

Mahoney, S. "Ten Secrets of a Good Long Life." *AARP The Magazine.* (July/August 2005): 46–53.

Oddgeir, F., Dag Barlaug, and Monica Martinussen, et al. "Resilience in Relation to Personality and Intelligence." *International Journal of Methods in Psychiatric Research* 14, no. 1 (2005): 29–42.

Reivich, Karen and Andrew Shatté. *The Resilience Factor: 7 Essential Skills for Overcoming Life's Inevitable Obstacles.* New York: Broadway Books, 2002.

Smith, H., M. Smith, and S. Smith. *101 Secrets for a Great Retirement: Practical, Inspirational and Fun Ideas for the Best Years of Your Life.* Los Angeles: Lowell House, 2000.

Watson, D., B. Hubbard, and D. Wiese. "General Traits of Personality and Affectivity as Predictors of Satisfaction in Intimate Relationships: Evidence from Self- and Partner-ratings." *Journal of Personality* 68 (2000): 413–49.

Watson, D., D. Wiese, and J. Vaidya, et al. "The Two General Activation Systems of Affect: Structural Findings, Evolutionary Considerations, and Psychobiological Evidence." *Journal of Personality* 76 (1999): 820–38.

CHAPTER SIX: TRAIT FOUR: A LITTLE HELP FROM YOUR FRIENDS (AND FAMILY)—THE STRONG SUPPORT GROUP

Acitelli, L. and T. Antonucci. "Reciprocity of Social Support in Older Married Couples." *Journal of Personality and Social Psychology* 67 (1994): 688–98.

Antonucci, T., and H. Akiyama. "Social Relationships and Aging Well." *Generations* 15 (1991): 43–59.

Calasanti, T. "Gender and Life Satisfaction in Retirement: An Assessment of the Male Model." *Journal of Gerontology Series B: Psychological Sciences and Social Sciences* 51 (1996): 18–29.

Cutrona, C., D. Russell, and J. Rose. "Social Support and Adaptation to Stress by the Elderly." *Psychology and Aging* 1 (1986): 47–54.

Fletcher, W., and R. Hansson. "Assessing the Social Components of Retirement Anxiety." *Psychology and Aging* 6, no. 1 (1991): 76–85.

Gordimer, Nadine. *Get a Life.* New York: Penguin, 2006, pp. 68–110.

Helen, M., and S. Smith. *101 Secrets for a Great Retirement; Practical, Inspirational, and Fun Ideas for the Best Years of Your Life.* Blacklick, Ohio: McGraw-Hill Companies/NTC Contemporary Publishing Group, no date, pp. 101–8.

Hooyman, N., and A. Kiyak. *Social Gerontology: A Multidisciplinary Perspective.* Needham Heights, Mass.: Allyn & Bacon, 2004.

Howard, Julie G., "Marital Dyads and Crossover Effects in Retirement Adjustment and Well-Being." Ph.D. diss., Portland State University, 2005.

Larson, R., R. Mannell, and J. Zuzanek. "Daily Well-Being of Older Adults with Friends and Family." *Psychology and Aging* 1 (1986): 117–26.

Polston, B. *Loving Midlife Marriage: A Guide to Keeping Romance Alive from the Empty Nest through Retirement.* New York: John Wiley & Sons, 1999, pp. 214–22.

Ray, D. *The Forty Plus Handbook: The Fine Art of Growing Older.* Nashville: W Publishing Group, 1979, pp. 63–97.

Rowe, John W., and Robert L. Kahn. *Successful Aging.* New York: Dell Publishing, 1999, pp. 97–120; 152–66.

Uhlenberg, P. "Essays on Age Integration." *The Gerontologist* 40, no. 3 (2000): 261–308.

Vinick, B., and D. Ekerdt. "Retirement and the Family." *Generations: Journal of the American Society on Aging* 13 (1989): 53–56.

Zelinski, E. *How to Retire Happy, Wild, and Free: Retirement Wisdom That You Won't Get from Your Financial Advisor.* Berkeley: Ten Speed Press, 2004, pp. 141–64.

Chapter Seven: Trait Five: Kick Back— Enjoy Leisure Time

Barnett, J. *How to Feel Good as You Age: A Voice of Experience.* Acton, Mass.: VanderWyk & Burnham, 2000.

Broderick T. and B. Glazer. "Leisure Participation and the Retirement Process." *American Journal of Occupational Therapy* 37, no. 1 (1983): 15–22.

Csikszentmihalyi, Mihaly. *Creativity: Flow and the Psychology of Discovery and Invention.* New York: HarperCollins, 1996.

Giffin J., and K. McKenna. "Influences on Leisure and Life Satisfaction of Elderly People." *Physical and Occupational Therapy in Geriatrics* 15, no. 4 (1998): 1–16.

Guinn B. "Leisure Behavior Motivation and the Life Satisfaction of Retired Persons." *Activities, Adaptation and Aging* 23, no. 4 (1999).

Hooyman, N., and A. Kiyak. *Social Gerontology: A Multidisciplinary Perspective.* Needham Heights, Mass.: Allyn & Bacon, 2004.

Kerr, Walter. *The Decline of Pleasure.* London: Touchstone, 1962.

Kujala, U. M., J. Kaprio, and S. Sarna, et al. "Relationship of Leisure Time Physical Activity and Mortality." *Journal of the American Medical Association* 279, no. 6 (1998): 438–43.

McGuire, F. A., F. D. Dottavio, and J. T. O'Leary. "The Relationship of Early Life Experiences to Later Life Leisure Involvement." *Leisure Sciences* 9, no. 4 (1987): 251–57.

Menec, V. H., and J. G. Chipperfield. "Remaining Active in Later Life: The Role of Locus of Control in Seniors' Leisure Activity Participation, Health and Life Satisfaction." *Journal of Aging and Health* 9, no. 1 (1997): 105–25.

Yamada, N. "The Relationship Between Leisure Activities, Psycho-Social Development and Life Satisfaction in Late Adulthood" [Japanese]. *Japanese Journal of Developmental Psychology* 11, no. 1 (2000): 34–44.

CHAPTER EIGHT: TRAIT SIX: HERE'S TO YOUR HEALTH

Boulé, Margie. "Go Ahead and Giggle: Laughter Really Is the Best (Ha-Ha) Medicine." *The Oregonian,* June 26, 2007.

Centers for Disease Control and Prevention. "Obesity and Overweight: Introduction," www.cdc.gov/nccdphp/dnpa/obesity/

Chang, Alicia. "Diets Fail in the Long Run, Study Says." The Associated Press, 2007.

Cronin-Stubbs, D. "Sick in Mind and Body." AARP Andrus Foundation. www.andrus.org/...l/latestresearch/ssi/healine4.html

Fabrigoule, C., L. Letenneur, and J. F. Dartigues, et al. "Social and Leisure Activities and Risk of Dementia: A Prospective Longitudinal Study." *Journal of the American Geriatrics Society* 43 (1995): 485–90.

Finch, C. E., and R. E. Tanzi. "Genetics of Aging." *Science* 278 (1997): 407–11.

"Gallup Poll, 2000." The Gallup Organization, www.gallup.com/poll/indicators/indalcohol.asp

Gilbaugh, J. H. *Men's Private Parts.* New York: Simon & Schuster, 2002.

Goldberg, Linn, and Diane L. Elliott. *The Healing Power of Exercise: Your Guide to*

Preventing and Treating Diabetes, Depression, Heart Disease, High Blood Pressure, Arthritis, and More. Hoboken, N.J.: John Wiley & Sons, Inc., 2000.

Goldberg, R. J., M. Larson, and D. Levy. "Factors Associated with Survival to 75 Years of Age in Middle-aged Men And Women." *Archives Internal Medicine* 156 (1996): 505–9.

Grant, W. "Incidence of Dementia and Alzheimer's Disease in Nigeria and the United States." *Journal of the American Medical Association* 285 (2001): 2448.

Johnson, S. *Who Moved My Cheese?* New York: G. P. Putnam's Sons, 1998.

Kolata, G. "Old But Not Frail: A Matter of Heart and Head." *The New York Times,* October 6, 2006, p. 1.

Larson, E. "Exercise Associates with Reduced Risk of Dementia in Older Adults." *Annals of Internal Medicine* 144 (2006):73–81.

Leitzmann, M., E. A. Platz, and J. S. Meir, et al. "Ejaculation Frequency and Subsequent Risk of Prostate Cancer." *Journal of the American Medical Association,* 291, 13 (2004): 1578–86.

Mann, T., A. J. Tomiyama, E. Lew, et al. "Medicare's Search for Effective Obesity Treatments: Diets are Not the Answer." *American Psychologist* 62, no. 3 (2007): 220–33.

Morris, M. "Consumption of Fish and Omega-3 Fatty Acids and Risk of Incident of Alzheimer's Disease." *Archives of Neurology* 60 (2003): 940–46.

Morris, M. "Dietary Fats and the Risk of Incident of Alzheimer's Disease." *Archives of Neurology* 60, no. 2 (2003): 194–200.

Morris, M. "Dietary Niacin and the Risk of Incident Alzheimer's Disease and of Cognitive Decline." *Journal of Neurology, Neurosurgery, and Psychiatry* 75, no. 8 (2004): 1093–99.

Paffenbarder, R. S., Jr., R. T. Hyde, and A. L. Wind, et al. "The Association of Changes in Physical Activity Level and Other Lifestyle Characteristics with Mortality Among Men." *New England Journal of Medicine* 328 (1993): 538–45.

Perls, Thomas, Margery Hutter Silver, and John F. Lauerman. *Living to 100: Lessons in Living to Your Maximum Potential at Any Age.* New York: Basic Books, 2000, pp. 155–210.

Reynolds, C. F., G. S. Alexopoulos, and I. R. Katz, et al. "Chronic Depression in the Elderly: Approaches for Prevention." *Drugs and Aging* 18, no. 7 (2001): 507–14.

Roizen, M. F. *Real Age: Are You as Young as You Can Be?* New York: Cliff Street Books, 1999.

Rosenfeld, I. *Live Now, Age Later: Proven Ways to Slow Down the Clock.* New York: Warner Books, 1999.

Ross, Emma. "Obese People Can Still Be Fit, Expert Says." *The Oregonian,* July 18, 2001, p. A9.

Rowe, John W. and Robert L. Kahn. *Successful Aging.* New York: Dell Publishing, 1999, pp. 97–120.

Smith, G. D., S. Frankel, and J. Yarnell. "Sex and Death: Are They Related? Findings from the Caerphilly Cohort Study." *British Medical Journal,* 315, no. 7123 (1997): 1641–44.

Sorlie, Paul D., Eric Backlund, and Jacob B. Keller. "U.S. Mortality by Economic, Demographic, and Social Characteristics: The National Longitudinal Mortality Study." *American Journal of Public Health* 85, no. 7 (1995): 949–56.

Spriegel, K., R. Leproult, and E. V. Cauter. "Impact of Sleep Debt on Metabolic and Endocrine Function." *The Lancet:* 354 (1999): 1435–39.

Takeuchi, J., and S. Groeneman. "'Stealing Time' Study: A Summary of Findings." Washington, D.C.: AARP Research Group, 1999.

Vaillant, G. E., and K. Mukarnal. "Successful Aging." *American Journal of Psychiatry:* 158 (2001): 839–47.

Weller, I., and P. Corey. "The Impact of Excluding Non-leisure Energy Expenditure on the Relation Between Physical Activity and Mortality in Women." *Epidemiology* 9 (1998): 632–35.

West, R. R. "Smoking: Its Influence on Survival and Cause of Death." *Journal of the Royal College of Physicians of London* 26, no. 4 (1992): 357–63.

CHAPTER NINE: TRAIT SEVEN: PASSION AND PURPOSE

Csikszentmihalyi, Mihaly. *Flow: The Psychology of Optimal Experience.* New York: Harper & Row, 1990.

Helen, M. and S. Smith. *101 Secrets for a Great Retirement.* Los Angeles: McGraw-Hill, 2000, pp. 1–157.

Hudson, F. M. *The Adult Years: Mastering the Art of Self-Renewal.* Revised edition. San Francisco: Jossey-Bass Publishers, 1999.

Leibowitz, M. "Charting a Course in Rough Financial Seas." TIAA-CREF Participant, May 2001, pp. 5–10.

Leider, Richard J., and David A. Shapiro. *Repacking Your Bags—Lighten Your Load for the Rest of Your Life.* San Francisco: Berrett-Koehler, 1995.

Older American 2000: Key Indicators of Well-Being. Federal Interagency Forum on Aging Related Statistics, 2000.

Stewart, Lisa. "So What Are You Doing with Yourself These Days?" NY., N.Y., PaineWebber, 1993.

CHAPTER TEN: TRAIT EIGHT: LET THE SPIRIT MOVE YOU—SPIRITUALITY AND RELIGION

Achenbaum, A., and S. Modell. "Joan and Erik Erikson and Sarah and Abraham: Parallel Awakenings in the Long Shadow of Wisdom and Faith." *Religion, Belief, and Spirituality in Late Life.* New York: Springer Publishing Company, 1999, pp. 13–24.

Birren, J., and K. Warner Schaie. *Handbook of the Psychology of Aging.* Oxford, U.K.: Elsevier Science, 2001.

Fowler, J. *Stages of Faith.* New York: Harper & Row. 1981, pp. 9–15.

"Gallup Poll, Religion." The Gallup Organization, 2006. www.galluppoll.com/content/default.aspx?ci=1690

Hooyman, N., and A. Kiyak. *Social Gerontology: A Multidisciplinary Perspective.* Needham Heights, Mass.: Allyn & Bacon, 2004.

James, William. *The Varieties of Religious Experience: A Study in Human Nature.* Centenary edition. London: Routledge, 2002.

Jewell, A. *Aging, Spirituality, and Well-Being.* London: Jessica Kingsley, 2003.

Koenig, H., L. George, and I. Siegler. "The Use of Religion and Other Emotion-Regulation Coping Strategies Among Older Adults." *Gerontologist* 28, no. 3 (June 1988): 303–10.

Levin, J. "Religion." *The Encyclopedia of Aging.* Second edition. New York: Springer Publishing Company, 1995, pp. 799–802.

Mitroff, I., and E. Denton. "A Study of Spirituality in the Workplace." *Sloan Management Review* (Summer 1999): 83–92.

Pascal, Blaise. www.oregonstate.edu/instruct/phl302/philosophers/pascal.html

Roof, W. C. *Spiritual Marketplace: Baby Boomers and the Remaking of American Religion.* Princeton, N.J.: Princeton University Press, 2001.

Thomas, L., and S. Eisenhandler. *Religion, Belief, and Spirituality in Late Life.* New York: Springer Publishing Company, 1999.

Tornstan, L. "Late-Life Transcendence: A New Developmental Perspective on Aging." *Religion, Belief, and Spirituality in Late Life.* New York: Springer Publishing Company, 1999.

Wink, P. "Addressing End-of-Life Issues: Spirituality and Inner Life." *Generations: Journal of the American Society on Aging* 23, no. 1 (Spring 1999). San Francisco: ASA Publications.

Wolfe, A. *The Transformation of American Religion: How We Actually Live Our Faith.* New York: Free Press, 2003.

Zinnbauer, B., K. Pargament, and B. Cole, et al. "Religion and Spirituality: Unfuzzying the Fuzzy." *Journal for the Scientific Study of Religion* 36, no. 4 (1997): 549–64.

CHAPTER ELEVEN: INTO THE FUTURE

Buford, Bob. *Game Plan—Winning Strategies for the Second Half of Your Life.* Grand Rapids: Zondervan Publishing House, 1999.

Carlson, B. "The New Rules of Retirement." *Bob Carlson's Retirement Watch,* Sep. 1–2, 2000.

Howard, Julie G. "Marital Dyads and Crossover Effects in Retirement Adjustment and Well-Being." Ph.D. diss., Portland State University, 2005.

Kolata, G. "Old But Not Frail: A Matter of Heart and Head." *The New York Times,* Oct. 6, 2006, p. 1.

Larsen, E. "The Occasional Volunteer." *AARP The Magazine,* January/February 2001, pp. 53–61.

Mahoney, Sara. "Ten Secrets of a Good Long Life." *AARP The Magazine,* July/August 2005, pp. 46–53.

Moen, P., W. A. Erickson, and M. Agarwal, et al. "Cornell Retirement and Well-Being Study Final Report." Ithaca, N.Y.: Bronfenbrenner Life Course Center, 2000.

Novelli, W. "Reinventing Retirement: Tell Us What You're Doing." *AARP The Magazine,* March 2002, p. 20.

RETIREMENT RESOURCES

HOUSING

Retire in Style: 60 Outstanding Places Across the USA and Canada by Warren R. Bland, Ph.D. (Chester, N.J.: Next Decade, Inc., 2002).

CAREGIVERS

American Medical Association Guide to Home Caregiving by the American Medical Association (New York: John Wiley & Sons, 2001).

The Caregiver's Essential Handbook: More than 1,200 Tips to Help You Care for and Comfort the Seniors in Your Life by Sasha Carr, M.S. (New York: McGraw-Hill, 2003).

The Comfort of Home: An Illustrated Step-by-Step Guide for Caregivers, 2nd Edition by Maria M. Meyer and Paula Derr, R.N. (Portland, Ore.: Care Trust Publications, 2002).

The Complete Eldercare Planner: Where to Start, Which Questions to Ask, and How to Find Help, 2nd Edition by Joy Loverde (New York: Three Rivers Press, 2000).

MENTAL HEALTH

The Healing Journey Through Retirement by Phil Rich, Ed.D., MSW, D. M.
Sampson, and D. S. Fetherling. (New York: John Wiley & Sons, 1999).

Transitions: Making Sense of Life's Changes by William Bridges, (New York: Da
Capo Press, 2004).

EDUCATION AND COMPUTERS

It's Never Too Late to Love a Computer: The Fearless Guide for Seniors by Abby
Stokes (New York: Workman Publishing, 2005).

Senior's Guide to Easy Computing: PC Basics, Internet, and E-mail by Rebecca
Sharp Colmer (Chelsea, Mich.: Eklektika Press, 2004).

VOLUNTEERING

The Power of Purpose: Living Well by Doing Good by Peter S. Temes (New York:
Three Rivers Press, 2007).

*Volunteering: The Selfish Benefits: Achieve Deep-Down Satisfaction and Create That
Desire in Others* by Charles A. Bennett (Oak View, Calif.: Committee Commu-
nications, 2001).

TRAVEL

Complete Guide to Full-Time RVing: Life on the Open Road by Bill and Jan Moeller
(Ventura, Calif.: Trailer Life Books, 1998).

*Have Grandchildren, Will Travel: The Hows and Wheres of a Glorious Vacation With
Your Children's Children* by Virginia Spurlock (New York: Pilot Books, 1997).

HEALTH AND FITNESS

Fitter After 50: Forever Changing Our Beliefs About Aging by Edwin Mayhew (Bloomington, Ind.: 1st Books Library, 2002).

STATISTICS

DESCRIPTION OF DATA ANALYSIS FOR RETIREMENT STUDY

All survey data were input and analyzed using the Statistical Package for the Social Sciences software. Chi-square analyses were conducted to identify group differences in categorical variables. For continuous variables, independent sample t-tests were used to identify differences between men and women, and between homemakers and working/retired women. To identify differences by group/stage/phase of work-retirement (the four groups), one-way analysis of variance and Scheffé post hoc comparisons were conducted.

The Retirement Quotient (RQ) was constructed using a combination of literature review and inductive and empirical methods. Possible indicators of perceived success in retirement were identified through a review of the literature and through the judgment of the investigators. Correlation analyses of each of these indicators with perceived retirement success were then conducted. Also, inter-item correlation analyses were conducted to determine indicators that were so highly correlated as to be essentially duplicative of each other. The resulting 22 indicators are those that constitute the RQ, with an alpha coefficient (reliability) of .75.

Multivariate analyses were also conducted. Specifically, using multiple linear regression, the 22 RQ indicators were entered into the equation simultaneously to determine which ones contributed the most to predicting perceived success in retirement.

This work was conducted by Margaret Beth Neal, Ph.D., director of the Institute on Aging, Portland State University.

INDEX